TABLE Q
CONTENTS

GREAT CITIES 2 QUART MEALS

Welcome America!

Welcome to a flavorful journey across America, designed for your mini 2-quart slow cooker. This book celebrates American cuisine with perfectly portioned recipes, ideal for individuals or couples. Each dish offers a taste of regional heritage, making it easy to explore the country's flavors from your kitchen.

Enjoy iconic dishes like Kansas City BBQ Sliders, Montana's Huckleberry BBQ Ribs, or Nebraska's Corn and Cheese Casserole. Savor Nevada's Lamb and Potato Stew, New Hampshire's Maple Pork & Sweet Potato Stew, or the comforting New Mexico Green Chile Chicken Stew. Try unique meals like New York's Reuben Casserole, Rhode Island's Corn and Clam Chowder, or Texas Brisket and Pinto Bean Chili. With cozy stews, hearty chilis, and bold BBQ, each recipe highlights the soulful depth of slow cooking. Tailored for your 2-quart slow cooker, these regional classics are scaled perfectly for your table. Let your slow cooker create comforting meals with ease, one pot at a time.

"*Good food and a warm kitchen are what make a house a home.*"

- Rachael Ray

This cookbook is designed for simplicity and flavor, offering recipes perfectly portioned for two servings. Whether you're cooking for a partner, a friend, or prefer minimal leftovers, these dishes are tailored to fit your needs. Each recipe features a vibrant photo to guide you, so you can see exactly how your meal will look when it's done.

The beauty of slow cooking lies in its ability to transform fresh ingredients into dishes that reflect the rich culinary traditions of America. Try Alabama's White BBQ Chicken or savor the hearty flavors of Alaska's Halibut and Potato Stew. Dive into the spicy comfort of Arizona's Chorizo and Green Chile Casserole, or enjoy the homestyle goodness of Arkansas's Buttermilk Chicken & Cornbread Bake.

From the vibrant California Avocado Citrus Chicken Bowls to the rustic Colorado Elk and Sweet Potato Hash, this book highlights the best of regional cuisine. Enjoy the sweetness of Georgia's Vidalia Onion and Peach Glazed Pork, the tropical flair of Hawaii's Pineapple Teriyaki Chicken, or the comforting richness of Idaho's Loaded Cheddar Potato Bake.

With your slow cooker handling the heavy lifting, you'll savor deeply developed flavors from across the U.S., one pot at a time. Let these easy, flavorful recipes bring America's diverse culinary heritage to your table!

"A recipe has no soul. You, as the cook, must bring soul to the recipe."

– Thomas Keller

Scan for FREE Coffee Book

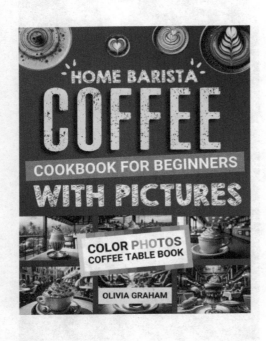

Scan to REVIEW this Book (Thanks)

Crockpot 2 Quart Basics

Essential Features and How to Use Them

The 2 Quart Crock Pot is compact yet versatile, with a simple design that focuses on ease of use. Its primary settings—Low, High, and Warm—give you the flexibility to cook a variety of dishes.

- **Low Setting:** This is your go-to for slow, all-day cooking. It's perfect for tough cuts of meat that benefit from long, gentle heat to become tender and flavorful. Cooking on low typically takes 6-8 hours, allowing flavors to meld beautifully.
- **High Setting:** For quicker cooking, the high setting reduces the cook time to about 2-4 hours. While it's faster, it still retains the slow-cooking essence, producing rich and savory results.
- **Warm Setting:** Once your food is cooked, switch to warm to maintain its temperature without overcooking. This is ideal for meals you're not serving immediately or for keeping dips and appetizers ready for guests.

To get started, load your ingredients into the removable stoneware, place the lid securely, and set the desired temperature. For optimal results, fill the crockpot between half and three-quarters full—this ensures even cooking and prevents spills. The stoneware insert and lid are typically dishwasher-safe, simplifying cleanup after your meal.

Tips for First-Time Slow Cookers

If you're new to slow cooking, don't worry—this simple yet powerful tool will quickly become your kitchen favorite. Here are some tips to get started:

- **Ingredient Prep:** Chop vegetables uniformly to ensure even cooking. Place harder vegetables, like carrots and potatoes, at the bottom since they take longer to cook, and layer softer ingredients on top.
- **Avoid Overfilling or Underfilling:** Overfilling can cause spills, while underfilling may lead to uneven cooking or dried-out dishes.
- **Minimize Lid Opening:** Resist the urge to check on your meal frequently. Each time the lid is lifted, heat escapes, adding 15-20 minutes to the cooking time.
- **Preheat When Possible:** Preheating the crockpot before adding ingredients can speed up cooking slightly and prevent a cold start.
- **Start Simple:** Begin with beginner-friendly recipes like soups, stews, or shredded chicken to familiarize yourself with cooking times and results.

Small-Batch Cooking Tips

Choosing the Right Ingredients for Small Batches

- Proteins: Choose boneless, skinless cuts like chicken breasts or thighs, or small portions of beef, pork, or fish that will cook evenly.
- Vegetables: Root vegetables like carrots, potatoes, and parsnips are ideal because they hold up well during long cooking times.
- Liquids: Slow cookers need moisture to prevent burning, but a 2-quart model requires less liquid than larger ones—typically half the amount called for in larger recipes.

Adjusting Recipes for a 2-Quart Crockpot

To adapt recipes for a smaller crockpot, scale down ingredient quantities while maintaining ratios:
- Divide ingredients by half or quarter, depending on the recipe's size.
- Keep an eye on cooking times; smaller batches may cook faster. Start checking for doneness about 30 minutes earlier than suggested.
- Reduce liquid amounts but ensure there's enough to cover the bottom of the crockpot to avoid scorching.

Layering Ingredients for Even Cooking

1. Dense Items First: Place root vegetables or other hard ingredients at the bottom, as they take the longest to cook.
2. Proteins Next: Add meat or beans on top of the vegetables.
3. Delicate Ingredients Last: Greens, herbs, or dairy-based additions should go in during the final 30 minutes to prevent overcooking.

Common Mistakes to Avoid

1. Overfilling or Underfilling: Fill your crockpot between 50-75% capacity for optimal cooking.
2. Skipping Preheating: Preheating can help your meal cook evenly and avoid temperature fluctuations.
3. Lifting the Lid: Every time you open the lid, you lose heat and add cooking time.
4. Using Frozen Ingredients: Thaw ingredients beforehand to ensure proper cooking and food safety.

Meal Prep and Planninig

How to Plan Weekly Meals with Your Crockpot

Start by assessing your schedule and selecting meals that align with your time and energy. For instance:
- Busy Weekdays: Opt for low-maintenance dishes like soups, stews, or shredded meats that can cook while you're away.
- Meal Variety: Avoid boredom by choosing diverse recipes—try a chili for one day, a creamy pasta dish for another, and a hearty vegetable stew midweek.
- Double Duty: Plan meals that yield leftovers or versatile components. For example, slow-cooked pulled chicken can serve as taco filling one night and a salad topping the next.

Once you've picked your recipes, create a shopping list and group ingredients by category (produce, meats, pantry items) to save time at the store. Prepping ingredients ahead ensures smoother cooking throughout the week.

Ingredient Prep Shortcuts

Efficient ingredient preparation can transform meal prep from a chore into a quick task:
- Chop in Advance: Dice vegetables like onions, carrots, and celery in batches and store them in airtight containers.
- Pre-Measure Spices: Combine seasonings for each recipe into small containers or bags to save time when assembling meals.
- Utilize Frozen Ingredients: Pre-chopped frozen veggies and herbs are time-savers. Just thaw slightly to reduce added moisture in your crockpot.
- Batch Cook Base Ingredients: Prepare grains, beans, or shredded proteins in bulk and portion them out for various meals during the week.

Make-Ahead Meals for Busy Days

For hectic days, assembling meals in advance can be a game-changer. Layer ingredients directly in a freezer-safe bag or container in the order they'll cook (e.g., hard vegetables on the bottom, proteins next, and sauces last). Store these pre-assembled meals in the freezer or fridge until ready to cook. On the day of cooking, simply transfer the contents to your crockpot and let it do the work.

Tips for Perfect Crockpot Cooking

When (and When Not) to Peek Inside

Every time you lift the lid, the internal temperature of your crockpot drops significantly, adding 15-20 minutes to the cooking time. For consistent results, avoid opening the lid unless absolutely necessary. The only time you should peek inside is toward the end of the cooking cycle to check doneness or stir, if the recipe specifies. Use a glass lid to monitor your food without disrupting the cooking process.

How to Prevent Overcooking in a Smaller Crockpot

Smaller crockpots, like the 2-quart model, tend to heat up more quickly than their larger counterparts due to their compact size. To prevent overcooking:
1. Follow recipes designed specifically for smaller slow cookers, as cooking times will already be adjusted.
2. Use a kitchen timer to check your food earlier than the recipe suggests.
3. Opt for the Warm setting once the dish is cooked to avoid drying out your meal, especially for soups or casseroles.

Adapting Recipes from Larger Crockpots to 2-Quart Models

You don't have to limit yourself to recipes written for smaller crockpots; adapting larger recipes is easy with a few adjustments:
1. Scale Ingredients: Reduce ingredient quantities by half or more to match your crockpot's capacity. Aim to fill it between 50-75% full for optimal cooking.
2. Adjust Cooking Times: Smaller portions often cook faster, so reduce cooking time by 20-30% and monitor doneness.
3. Maintain Ratios: Keep the balance of liquids and solids consistent to ensure the dish cooks properly and doesn't dry out or become too watery.

Using Liners and Other Tools for Easy Cleanup

Crockpot liners are a game-changer for hassle-free cleanup. These disposable, heat-safe bags fit inside the stoneware and prevent food from sticking. After cooking, simply remove the liner and dispose of it.
Other useful tools include:
- Silicone Spatulas: Gentle on the crockpot surface and perfect for stirring.
- Small Whisks: Ideal for mixing sauces or gravies directly in the crockpot.
- Portion Scoops: Handy for dividing leftovers into small servings.

Special Considerations for Crockpot Cooking

Cooking Times for Various Ingredients

Cooking times vary depending on the type of ingredient and the setting used (Low vs. High).

- Vegetables:
  - Root Vegetables (e.g., carrots, potatoes, turnips): These take the longest to cook, often 6-8 hours on Low or 3-5 hours on High.
  - Tender Vegetables (e.g., zucchini, spinach, bell peppers): Add these in the last 30-45 minutes of cooking to prevent them from becoming mushy.
- Proteins:
  - Chicken: Boneless, skinless cuts cook in 6-8 hours on Low or 3-4 hours on High. Bone-in chicken may take slightly longer.
  - Beef and Pork: Tough cuts like chuck roast or pork shoulder are ideal for slow cooking, taking 8-10 hours on Low or 4-6 hours on High.
  - Fish and Seafood: These cook quickly and should be added during the final hour to avoid overcooking.
- Grains and Legumes:
  - Grains: Pre-cooked grains like rice or quinoa should be stirred in during the last 20-30 minutes to avoid overcooking. Alternatively, use the crockpot's warm setting to finish them.
  - Legumes: Soaked beans cook in 6-8 hours on Low, while lentils require less time (4-6 hours on Low).

Doubling Recipes: What Works and What Doesn't

Doubling recipes in a crockpot can be tricky, especially in smaller models like a 2-quart crockpot.

- What Works:
  - Soups and stews are easily scalable. Just ensure you don't overfill the crockpot; it should only be filled between 50-75% capacity for even cooking.
  - Protein-based recipes (like shredded chicken or pulled pork) also work well when doubled, as the slow cooker evenly distributes heat.
- What Doesn't Work:
  - Recipes that rely on precise layering (e.g., lasagna or casseroles) can lose their structure when doubled. Instead, cook these in batches.
  - Baked goods, like slow-cooker cakes or bread, may not cook evenly when doubled due to the increased volume.
  - Liquid-heavy recipes can become overly watery. When doubling, reduce the liquid slightly, as the slow cooker retains moisture during cooking.

White BBQ Chicken

Alabama

To make perfect White BBQ Chicken for one or two people in a mini 2-quart crock pot, use chicken thighs or breasts, as they retain moisture well. Sear the chicken briefly before adding it to the slow cooker for extra flavor. Add the white BBQ sauce toward the end of cooking to avoid breaking the creamy consistency. Use high for 2-3 hours or low for 4-5 hours until the chicken is tender. Baste the chicken with sauce every hour if possible. Pair with a side of cornbread or slaw for a classic Alabama meal.

Ingredients

1/2 cup mayonnaise, 2 tbsp apple cider vinegar, 1 tsp Dijon mustard, 1/2 tsp horseradish, 1/2 tsp sugar, 1/4 tsp garlic powder, 1/4 tsp onion powder, 1/4 tsp salt, 1/4 tsp black pepper, 1 lb boneless, skinless chicken thighs or breasts.

Preparation

- Mix mayonnaise, apple cider vinegar, Dijon mustard, horseradish, sugar, garlic powder, onion powder, salt, and black pepper in a small bowl to create the white BBQ sauce.
- Lightly sear chicken thighs or breasts in a skillet over medium heat to lock in juices and flavor.
- Place the chicken in the mini 2-quart crock pot.
- Pour half the white BBQ sauce over the chicken, reserving the other half for serving.
- Set the crock pot to low for 4-5 hours or high for 2-3 hours until the chicken is tender and cooked through.
- Baste chicken with the sauce every hour for extra flavor.
- Serve the chicken with reserved sauce and enjoy with traditional Southern sides.

Halibut and Potato Stew

Alaska

For a perfect Halibut and Potato Stew for one or two people in a mini 2-quart crock pot, use fresh halibut and cut it into chunks to ensure even cooking. Add the halibut in the final hour to prevent it from overcooking and falling apart. Use Yukon Gold potatoes, which hold their shape well. Cook the base of the stew (broth and vegetables) on low for 4-5 hours or high for 2-3 hours. Stir in cream and fresh dill during the last 30 minutes for a velvety texture. Serve with crusty bread for a hearty Alaskan experience.

Ingredients

1 1/2 lb halibut fillet, 1/4 cup flour, 1/4 cup panko breadcrumbs, 1/2 lb halibut fillet, 1 1/2 cups Yukon Gold potatoes (diced), 1/4 cup onion (chopped), 1/4 cup celery (diced), 1 cup fish or chicken broth, 1/4 tsp garlic powder, 1/4 tsp salt, 1/4 tsp pepper, 1/4 cup heavy cream, 1 tsp fresh dill (chopped).

Preparation

- Peel and dice Yukon Gold potatoes into small cubes, and chop onion and celery.
- Add potatoes, onion, celery, fish or chicken broth, garlic powder, salt, and pepper to the mini 2-quart crock pot.
- Set the crock pot to low for 4-5 hours or high for 2-3 hours, until the potatoes are tender.
- Cut the halibut fillet into bite-sized chunks. Add the halibut to the crock pot during the final hour of cooking.
- Stir in the heavy cream and chopped dill during the last 30 minutes, ensuring the stew is well-mixed.
- Serve hot, garnished with additional dill if desired, alongside a slice of crusty bread.

Chorizo and Green Chile Casserole

Arizona

To prepare a perfect Chorizo and Green Chile Casserole in a mini 2-quart crock pot, use fresh chorizo and roasted Hatch green chiles for authentic flavors. Layer tortilla strips, chorizo, green chiles, and cheese evenly to ensure proper cooking. Start with a thin layer of sauce at the bottom to prevent sticking. Cook on low for 3-4 hours, checking for melted cheese and tender tortilla strips. Add fresh cilantro or a dollop of sour cream just before serving for a flavorful garnish. Serve this casserole with a side of refried beans or rice for a hearty and satisfying meal.

Ingredients

1/2 lb chorizo (cooked and crumbled), 4 oz green chiles (roasted and diced), 1/2 cup shredded cheddar cheese, 1/2 cup shredded Monterey Jack cheese, 4 small corn tortillas (cut into strips), 1/2 cup enchilada sauce, 1 tbsp chopped cilantro.

Preparation

- Cook the chorizo in a skillet until fully browned and crumbled, then drain excess grease.
- Layer 1/4 cup enchilada sauce at the bottom of the crock pot to prevent sticking.
- Add a layer of tortilla strips, followed by half of the chorizo, half the green chiles, and a mix of cheddar and Monterey Jack cheeses.
- Repeat the layering process, finishing with a layer of cheese on top.
- Cover and cook on low for 3-4 hours, until the cheese is melted and bubbly.
- Sprinkle chopped cilantro on top before serving, and enjoy with sour cream if desired.

Buttermilk Chicken and Cornbread Bake

Arkansas

To make a perfect Buttermilk Chicken and Cornbread Bake for one or two people in a mini 2-quart crock pot, marinate the chicken in buttermilk overnight for tenderness. Use pre-mixed cornbread batter for convenience and layer it over the chicken for even cooking. Cook on low for 3-4 hours, checking for a golden-brown crust on the cornbread. Avoid overmixing the batter to keep it fluffy. Add a drizzle of honey and fresh parsley before serving for a touch of sweetness and color. Serve alongside Southern-style greens or mashed potatoes for a complete Arkansas-inspired meal.

Ingredients

1/2 lb boneless, skinless chicken thighs, 1/2 cup buttermilk, 1/4 cup cornmeal mix, 1/4 cup milk, 1/4 cup shredded cheddar cheese, 1 tbsp honey, 1/2 tsp garlic powder, 1/4 tsp salt, 1/4 tsp black pepper, 1/4 tsp paprika, 1 tbsp fresh parsley (chopped).

Preparation

- Marinate chicken thighs in buttermilk, garlic powder, salt, black pepper, and paprika for at least 2 hours or overnight.
- Lightly grease the bottom of the crock pot with cooking spray. Place the marinated chicken in a single layer.
- In a bowl, mix cornmeal mix, milk, and shredded cheddar cheese until just combined.
- Pour the cornbread batter evenly over the chicken in the crock pot.
- Cover and cook on low for 3-4 hours, or until the cornbread is golden brown and cooked through.
- Drizzle honey over the cornbread and sprinkle with chopped parsley before serving.
- Serve warm with your favorite Southern sides for a comforting meal.

Avocado Citrus Chicken Bowls

Califonia

CALIFORNIA REPUBLIC

To prepare Avocado Citrus Chicken Bowls for one or two people in a mini 2-quart crock pot, use boneless, skinless chicken breasts for tender and juicy results. Season the chicken with citrus zest and cook in a mix of orange juice and chicken broth for a bright, flavorful base. Cook on low for 3-4 hours or high for 1.5-2 hours until the chicken shreds easily. Prepare quinoa separately for a fluffy texture, then layer with chicken, avocado, and orange slices. Add lime juice and fresh cilantro as a final touch. Serve immediately for a vibrant, fresh California-inspired meal.

Ingredients

1/2 lb boneless, skinless chicken breast, 1/2 cup orange juice, 1/4 cup chicken broth, 1/4 tsp garlic powder, 1/4 tsp paprika, 1/4 tsp salt, 1/4 tsp pepper, 1 cup cooked quinoa, 1/2 avocado (sliced), 1/2 orange (segmented), 1 tbsp fresh cilantro (chopped), 1 lime wedge.

Preparation

- Season chicken breasts with garlic powder, paprika, salt, and pepper for flavor.
- Place the seasoned chicken in the mini 2-quart crock pot and pour in the orange juice and chicken broth.
- Cover and set the crock pot to low for 3-4 hours or high for 1.5-2 hours until the chicken is tender and fully cooked.
- Once cooked, remove the chicken from the crock pot and shred it using two forks. Return the shredded chicken to the crock pot and mix it with the flavorful juices.
- Prepare quinoa separately according to package instructions, ensuring it is fluffy and warm.
- To assemble, spoon cooked quinoa into serving bowls.
- Top the quinoa with shredded chicken, layering evenly.
- Add slices of fresh avocado and orange segments for brightness.
- Garnish with chopped cilantro and a squeeze of lime juice for a fresh finish.

Elk and Sweet Potato Hash

Colorado

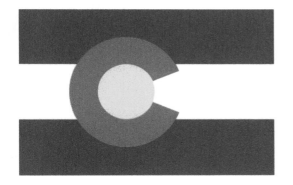

To make perfect Elk and Sweet Potato Hash for one or two people in a mini 2-quart crock pot, use tender elk stew meat and sweet potatoes for a flavorful base. Brown the elk meat in a skillet before adding it to the crock pot to enhance flavor. Layer the ingredients evenly, and cook on low for 6-7 hours or high for 3-4 hours, until the elk is tender and the sweet potatoes are soft but not mushy. Stir gently before serving to maintain texture. Garnish with fresh thyme for a fragrant finish, and serve with a fried egg on top for a hearty, mountain-inspired meal.

Ingredients

1/2 lb elk stew meat (cubed), 1 cup sweet potatoes (peeled and diced), 1/4 cup onion (chopped), 1/4 cup red bell pepper (diced), 1 tbsp olive oil, 1/2 tsp garlic powder, 1/4 tsp smoked paprika, 1/4 tsp salt, 1/4 tsp black pepper, 1/2 cup beef broth, 1 tsp fresh thyme (chopped).

Preparation

- Heat olive oil in a skillet and brown the elk stew meat for 2-3 minutes on each side to enhance flavor.
- Peel and dice the sweet potatoes into small, uniform pieces. Chop the onion and red bell pepper.
- Layer the browned elk meat at the bottom of the mini 2-quart crock pot, followed by sweet potatoes, onion, and red bell pepper.
- Sprinkle garlic powder, smoked paprika, salt, and black pepper evenly over the ingredients.
- Pour beef broth over the mixture to keep it moist and flavorful during cooking.
- Cover and cook on low for 6-7 hours or high for 3-4 hours, until the elk is tender and the sweet potatoes are soft.
- Stir gently to combine the flavors without breaking the sweet potatoes.
- Serve hot, garnished with fresh thyme, and enjoy with a fried egg if desired

Maple Dijon Pork Loin

Connecticut Ingredients

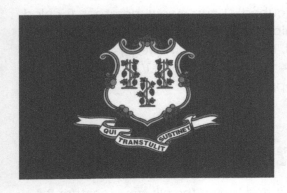

3/4 lb pork loin, 2 tbsp pure maple syrup, 1 tbsp Dijon mustard, 1 tbsp apple cider vinegar, 1/4 tsp garlic powder, 1/4 tsp smoked paprika, 1/4 tsp salt, 1/4 tsp black pepper, 1/4 cup chicken broth, 1 tsp fresh rosemary (chopped).

Preparation

To make perfect Maple Dijon Pork Loin for one or two people in a mini 2-quart crock pot, select a small, evenly-sized pork loin to ensure uniform cooking. Sear the pork in a skillet before slow cooking to develop a caramelized crust. Use pure maple syrup and a good-quality Dijon mustard for a well-balanced glaze. Cook on low for 5-6 hours or high for 2.5-3 hours until tender. Baste the pork with the maple-Dijon glaze during the last hour for extra flavor. Let the meat rest for 10 minutes before slicing to retain its juices. Serve with roasted vegetables or mashed potatoes for a comforting Connecticut-inspired meal.

- Season the pork loin with garlic powder, smoked paprika, salt, and black pepper.
- Heat a skillet over medium heat and sear the pork loin for 2-3 minutes on each side until browned.
- Place the pork loin in the mini 2-quart crock pot.
- In a small bowl, whisk together maple syrup, Dijon mustard, apple cider vinegar, and chicken broth. Pour the mixture over the pork loin.
- Cover and cook on low for 5-6 hours or high for 2.5-3 hours until the pork is tender and fully cooked.
- During the last hour of cooking, baste the pork with the glaze in the crock pot to enhance flavor.
- Once done, let the pork rest for 10 minutes, then slice and serve garnished with chopped rosemary.
- Pair with roasted vegetables or mashed potatoes for a complete meal.

Chicken and Slippery Dumplings

Delaware

DECEMBER 7, 1787

For a perfect Chicken and Slippery Dumplings recipe for one or two people in a mini 2-quart crock pot, use boneless chicken thighs for tender, flavorful results. Prepare the dumplings separately to ensure they stay intact and maintain their texture. Cook the chicken and broth base on low for 4-5 hours or high for 2-3 hours to achieve a rich, savory flavor. Add the dumplings during the last hour of cooking to absorb the broth without disintegrating. Garnish with fresh parsley for a finishing touch. Serve hot for a comforting and traditional Delaware meal.

Ingredients

1/2 lb boneless, skinless chicken thighs, 2 cups chicken broth, 1/4 cup diced onion, 1/4 cup diced celery, 1/2 cup all-purpose flour, 1/4 tsp baking powder, 1/4 tsp salt, 1 tbsp butter, 1/4 cup milk, 1/4 tsp black pepper, 1 tsp fresh parsley (chopped).

Preparation

- Dice the chicken thighs into small pieces and season with salt and black pepper.
- Add chicken, onion, celery, and chicken broth to the mini 2-quart crock pot. Stir to combine.
- Cover and cook on low for 4-5 hours or high for 2-3 hours, until the chicken is fully cooked and tender.
- Meanwhile, prepare the dumplings by mixing flour, baking powder, and salt in a bowl.
- Cut in butter until the mixture resembles coarse crumbs, then add milk and mix until a soft dough forms.
- Drop spoonfuls of the dough into the crock pot during the last hour of cooking.
- Cover and cook until dumplings are fluffy and cooked through, about 1 hour.
- Serve hot, garnished with chopped parsley, for a classic Delaware dish.

Mango and Black Bean Chicken

Florida

To prepare perfect Mango and Black Bean Chicken in a mini 2-quart crock pot, use fresh mango for natural sweetness and balance it with savory black beans. Dice the mango into small pieces to distribute flavor evenly. Cook the chicken on low for 4-5 hours or high for 2.5-3 hours until tender and easily shredded. Add the mango and beans during the last hour of cooking to preserve their texture. Garnish with fresh cilantro and lime for a refreshing finish. Serve over rice or quinoa for a complete Florida-inspired meal that's sweet, savory, and satisfying.

Ingredients

1/2 lb boneless, skinless chicken breast, 1/2 cup mango (diced), 1/2 cup black beans (canned, rinsed), 1/4 cup diced red bell pepper, 1/2 cup chicken broth, 1 tbsp lime juice, 1 tsp honey, 1/4 tsp garlic powder, 1/4 tsp cumin, 1/4 tsp salt, 1/4 tsp black pepper, 1 tsp fresh cilantro (chopped).

Preparation

- Season the chicken breast with garlic powder, cumin, salt, and black pepper.
- Place the chicken in the mini 2-quart crock pot. Add chicken broth, honey, and lime juice.
- Cover and cook on low for 4-5 hours or high for 2.5-3 hours until the chicken is tender.
- Dice the mango and red bell pepper into small pieces. Rinse and drain the canned black beans.
- During the last hour of cooking, add the mango, black beans, and red bell pepper to the crock pot. Stir gently.
- Once cooked, shred the chicken using two forks and mix it with the sauce and ingredients.
- Serve over rice or quinoa, garnished with chopped fresh cilantro and an additional squeeze of lime juice.

Vidalia Onion and Peach Glazed Pork

Georgia

To prepare Vidalia Onion and Peach Glazed Pork for one or two people in a mini 2-quart crock pot, use boneless pork chops for even cooking. Caramelize Vidalia onions before adding them for a rich flavor base. Cook the pork on low for 4-5 hours or high for 2.5-3 hours to ensure tenderness. Add the peach preserves in the last hour to prevent burning and to maintain a vibrant glaze. Garnish with fresh thyme for an aromatic finish. Serve alongside roasted vegetables or mashed sweet potatoes to complement the sweet and savory flavors of this Georgia-inspired dish.

Ingredients

1/2 lb boneless pork chops, 1/2 cup Vidalia onions (sliced), 2 tbsp peach preserves, 1/4 cup chicken broth, 1 tbsp balsamic vinegar, 1/4 tsp garlic powder, 1/4 tsp smoked paprika, 1/4 tsp salt, 1/4 tsp black pepper, 1 tsp fresh thyme (chopped), 1 tbsp butter.

Preparation

- Season the pork chops with garlic powder, smoked paprika, salt, and black pepper.
- Heat butter in a skillet and caramelize Vidalia onions until golden brown, about 5 minutes.
- Transfer the onions to the mini 2-quart crock pot and layer the pork chops on top.
- Mix chicken broth and balsamic vinegar, and pour over the pork and onions.
- Cover and cook on low for 4-5 hours or high for 2.5-3 hours until the pork is tender.
- During the last hour of cooking, spread peach preserves over the pork chops to create a glaze.
- Remove pork chops and onions carefully, spoon the glaze over the top, and garnish with fresh thyme.
- Serve warm with roasted vegetables or mashed sweet potatoes for a comforting Georgia-inspired meal.

Pineapple Teriyaki Chicken

Hawaii

For perfect Pineapple Teriyaki Chicken for one or two people in a mini 2-quart crock pot, use boneless, skinless chicken thighs for maximum flavor and tenderness. Combine fresh pineapple with teriyaki sauce for a tangy and sweet glaze. Cook on low for 4-5 hours or high for 2.5-3 hours until the chicken is tender. Add the pineapple chunks during the last hour to prevent them from becoming too mushy. Garnish with sesame seeds and green onions for added texture and flavor. Serve over steamed rice or noodles to complete this Hawaiian-inspired meal that's both tropical and satisfying.

Ingredients

1/2 lb boneless, skinless chicken thighs, 1/2 cup fresh pineapple chunks, 1/4 cup teriyaki sauce, 1 tbsp soy sauce, 1 tbsp honey, 1/4 tsp garlic powder, 1/4 tsp ginger powder, 1/4 tsp salt, 1/4 tsp black pepper, 1 tsp sesame seeds, 1 tbsp green onion (chopped).

Preparation

- Season the chicken thighs with garlic powder, ginger powder, salt, and black pepper.
- Place the chicken thighs in the mini 2-quart crock pot.
- In a small bowl, mix teriyaki sauce, soy sauce, and honey, then pour the mixture over the chicken.
- Cover and cook on low for 4-5 hours or high for 2.5-3 hours until the chicken is tender and cooked through.
- Add fresh pineapple chunks during the last hour of cooking to retain their texture and sweetness.
- Once cooked, remove the chicken and shred or leave whole, as preferred.
- Serve over steamed rice, spoon the pineapple-teriyaki sauce over the top, and garnish with sesame seeds and green onions.
- Enjoy a tropical taste of Hawaii in every bite.

Loaded Cheddar Potato Bake

Idaho

To create the perfect Loaded Cheddar Potato Bake for one or two people in a mini 2-quart crock pot, use Russet or Yukon Gold potatoes for their rich flavor and creamy texture. Thinly slice the potatoes evenly to ensure even cooking. Layer potatoes with cheddar cheese, bacon, and green onions for a balanced bite. Cook on low for 4-5 hours or high for 2.5-3 hours until the potatoes are tender and the cheese is melted. Avoid overcooking to preserve the layers' texture. Garnish with a dollop of sour cream and more green onions before serving for a hearty Idaho-inspired dish.

Ingredients

1 lb potatoes (sliced thinly), 1/2 cup shredded cheddar cheese, 2 slices cooked bacon (crumbled), 1/4 cup chopped green onions, 1/4 cup sour cream, 1 tbsp butter, 1/4 tsp garlic powder, 1/4 tsp salt, 1/4 tsp black pepper, 2 tbsp milk.

Preparation

- Peel and thinly slice the potatoes. Cook and crumble the bacon, and chop green onions.
- Grease the bottom of the mini 2-quart crock pot with butter. Layer half of the sliced potatoes on the bottom.
- Sprinkle garlic powder, salt, and pepper over the potato layer. Add half the shredded cheese, bacon, and green onions.
- Repeat with the remaining potatoes, seasonings, cheese, bacon, and green onions.
- Pour milk evenly over the layers to keep the dish moist during cooking.
- Cover and cook on low for 4-5 hours or high for 2.5-3 hours until the potatoes are tender and the cheese is melted.
- Serve warm, garnished with sour cream and additional green onions .

Chicago-Style Italian Sausage and Peppers

Illinois

Ingredients

2 Italian sausage links, 1/2 cup marinara sauce, 1/2 cup sliced bell peppers (red and green), 1/4 cup sliced onion, 1/4 tsp garlic powder, 1/4 tsp Italian seasoning, 1 tbsp olive oil, 1 tbsp grated Parmesan cheese, 2 hoagie rolls (optional).

Preparation

ILLINOIS

For an authentic Chicago-Style Italian Sausage and Peppers dish in a mini 2-quart crock pot, use high-quality Italian sausage and fresh bell peppers. Brown the sausages before slow cooking to lock in flavor. Add onions, peppers, and a rich tomato-based sauce for a hearty, flavorful meal. Cook on low for 4-5 hours or high for 2.5-3 hours until the sausages are tender. Serve on toasted hoagie rolls or over a bed of pasta. Garnish with Parmesan cheese or fresh parsley for a finishing touch.

- Heat olive oil in a skillet and brown the Italian sausages on all sides for about 3 minutes.
- Place the sausages in the mini 2-quart crock pot.
- Add sliced bell peppers and onions on top of the sausages.
- Sprinkle garlic powder and Italian seasoning evenly over the ingredients.
- Pour marinara sauce over the sausages and vegetables to coat evenly.
- Cover and cook on low for 4-5 hours or high for 2.5-3 hours until the sausages are fully cooked and tender.
- If serving with hoagie rolls, toast the rolls in the oven or on a skillet.
- Serve the sausages and peppers on hoagie rolls or over pasta, garnished with grated Parmesan cheese.
- Enjoy this hearty Illinois classic hot and fresh from the crock pot.

Hoosier Pork and Noodles

Indiana

For a perfect Hoosier Pork and Noodles dish in a mini 2-quart crock pot, use boneless pork shoulder for tender, flavorful meat. Cut the pork into bite-sized pieces for even cooking. Add egg noodles during the last 30 minutes to prevent overcooking. Cook on low for 6-7 hours or high for 3-4 hours until the pork is fork-tender. Stir in a splash of cream at the end for a rich, silky sauce. Garnish with fresh parsley for a touch of brightness. Serve with crusty bread or a side of green beans for a hearty Midwestern meal that's pure comfort food.

Ingredients

1/2 lb boneless pork shoulder (cubed), 1 cup chicken broth, 1/2 cup wide egg noodles, 1/4 cup diced onion, 1/4 cup diced celery, 1/4 tsp garlic powder, 1/4 tsp salt, 1/4 tsp black pepper, 1 tbsp heavy cream, 1 tsp fresh parsley (chopped).

Preparation

- Season the cubed pork with garlic powder, salt, and black pepper.
- Heat a skillet over medium heat and brown the pork on all sides for 3-4 minutes.
- Place the browned pork in the mini 2-quart crock pot. Add diced onion, celery, and chicken broth.
- Cover and cook on low for 6-7 hours or high for 3-4 hours until the pork is tender.
- During the last 30 minutes of cooking, stir in the wide egg noodles, ensuring they are submerged in the broth.
- Stir in the heavy cream just before serving to create a creamy sauce.
- Serve hot, garnished with fresh parsley, alongside crusty bread or a green vegetable for a balanced meal.

Sweet Corn and Bacon Chowder

Iowa

To make perfect Sweet Corn and Bacon Chowder in a mini 2-quart crock pot, use fresh or frozen corn for a naturally sweet flavor. Crisp the bacon beforehand to add smoky depth. Add potatoes for a hearty texture, and mix in cream during the last hour to prevent curdling. Cook on low for 4-5 hours to let the flavors meld. Garnish with extra bacon bits and fresh parsley before serving. Serve with crusty bread for a comforting Midwestern meal. This chowder celebrates Iowa's rich corn-growing tradition with its creamy, flavorful base and tender chunks of sweet corn.

Ingredients

1/2 cup corn kernels (fresh or frozen), 1/2 cup diced potatoes, 1/4 cup chopped onion, 1/4 cup diced celery, 1/4 cup heavy cream, 1/2 cup chicken broth, 2 slices bacon (cooked and crumbled), 1/4 tsp garlic powder, 1/4 tsp salt, 1/4 tsp black pepper, 1 tsp fresh parsley (chopped).

Preparation

- Cook the bacon in a skillet until crispy, then crumble and set aside. Reserve 1 tbsp of bacon grease.
- Add the reserved bacon grease, diced onion, and celery to the skillet and sauté until softened, about 3 minutes.
- Transfer the sautéed vegetables to the mini 2-quart crock pot.
- Add the corn kernels, diced potatoes, chicken broth, garlic powder, salt, and black pepper. Stir to combine.
- Cover and cook on low for 4-5 hours or high for 2-3 hours until the potatoes are tender.
- During the last hour, stir in the heavy cream and half of the crumbled bacon.
- Serve hot, garnished with the remaining bacon and fresh parsley. Pair with crusty bread for a complete meal.

Honey-Glazed Chicken Thighs

Kansas

For perfectly tender Honey-Glazed Chicken Thighs in a mini 2-quart crock pot, use bone-in chicken thighs for added flavor. Sear the thighs in a skillet first to enhance the caramelized glaze. Combine honey, garlic, and soy sauce for a sweet-savory marinade that infuses the chicken during slow cooking. Cook on low for 5-6 hours or high for 2.5-3 hours until the chicken is tender and glazed. Baste the chicken with the sauce every hour for an extra layer of flavor. Garnish with fresh thyme for a herbal touch and serve alongside roasted vegetables or mashed potatoes for a hearty Kansas-inspired meal.

Ingredients

1/2 lb bone-in chicken thighs, 2 tbsp honey, 1 tbsp soy sauce, 1 tbsp ketchup, 1/2 tsp garlic powder, 1/4 tsp smoked paprika, 1/4 tsp salt, 1/4 tsp black pepper, 1 tsp fresh thyme (chopped), 1/4 cup chicken broth.

Preparation

- Season the chicken thighs with garlic powder, smoked paprika, salt, and black pepper.
- Heat a skillet over medium heat and sear the chicken thighs for 2-3 minutes on each side until golden brown.
- Place the chicken in the mini 2-quart crock pot.
- In a small bowl, mix honey, soy sauce, ketchup, and chicken broth. Pour the mixture over the chicken.
- Cover and cook on low for 5-6 hours or high for 2.5-3 hours until the chicken is tender and glazed.
- During cooking, baste the chicken with the sauce every hour to enhance the flavor and glaze.
- Serve the chicken thighs warm, garnished with fresh thyme, alongside roasted vegetables or your favorite side dish.
- Enjoy a flavorful, Kansas-inspired meal that's sweet, savory, and comforting.

Bourbon-Glazed Short Ribs

Kentucky

For the perfect Bourbon-Glazed Short Ribs in a mini 2-quart crock pot, use meaty beef short ribs and a high-quality bourbon. Sear the ribs in a skillet before slow cooking to lock in flavor and create a caramelized crust. Cook on low for 6-8 hours or high for 4-5 hours until the ribs are tender and falling off the bone. Add the bourbon glaze in the last hour to enhance the flavor without overcooking the sauce. Serve with mashed potatoes or roasted vegetables for a complete Southern-inspired meal. Garnish with fresh parsley for a touch of brightness.

Ingredients

1 lb beef short ribs, 1/4 cup bourbon, 1/4 cup brown sugar, 1/4 cup beef broth, 1 tbsp soy sauce, 1 tbsp ketchup, 1/4 tsp garlic powder, 1/4 tsp onion powder, 1/4 tsp smoked paprika, 1 tbsp olive oil, 1 tsp fresh parsley (chopped).

Preparation

- Heat olive oil in a skillet over medium heat. Sear the short ribs for 2-3 minutes on each side until browned.
- Transfer the short ribs to the mini 2-quart crock pot.
- In a small bowl, mix bourbon, brown sugar, beef broth, soy sauce, ketchup, garlic powder, onion powder, and smoked paprika.
- Pour the bourbon mixture over the ribs, ensuring they are evenly coated.
- Cover and cook on low for 6-8 hours or high for 4-5 hours, until the ribs are tender and the meat easily falls off the bone.
- During the last hour of cooking, baste the ribs with the sauce in the crock pot to create a thick, flavorful glaze.
- Serve the ribs hot, garnished with fresh parsley, alongside mashed potatoes or roasted vegetables.
- Enjoy a rich, Southern-inspired meal with bold flavors.

Crawfish Étouffée

Lousiana

For authentic Crawfish Étouffée in a mini 2-quart crock pot, use fresh or frozen crawfish tails for the best flavor. Make a roux using butter and flour as the base for a rich, creamy texture. Add the holy trinity of Cajun cooking—bell peppers, onions, and celery—for depth. Cook on low for 4-5 hours to blend the flavors, adding the crawfish during the last 30 minutes to prevent overcooking. Serve over fluffy white rice and garnish with parsley. Adjust the spice level with hot sauce or cayenne pepper to suit your preference. Enjoy this Louisiana classic with a side of crusty French bread.

Ingredients

1/2 lb crawfish tails (peeled), 2 tbsp butter, 2 tbsp all-purpose flour, 1/2 cup diced onion, 1/4 cup diced celery, 1/4 cup diced bell pepper, 1 cup chicken broth, 1/4 tsp garlic powder, 1/4 tsp paprika, 1/8 tsp cayenne pepper, 1 tbsp fresh parsley (chopped), 1 cup cooked white rice.

Preparation

- In a skillet, melt butter over medium heat and whisk in the flour. Cook for 2-3 minutes, stirring constantly, until the roux is golden brown.
- Transfer the roux to the mini 2-quart crock pot. Add onion, celery, and bell pepper.
- Stir in chicken broth, garlic powder, paprika, and cayenne pepper. Mix well to combine.
- Cover and cook on low for 4-5 hours or high for 2-3 hours until the vegetables are tender and the sauce thickens.
- Add the crawfish tails during the last 30 minutes of cooking to prevent them from becoming rubbery.
- Taste and adjust seasoning if necessary.
- Serve the étouffée hot over cooked white rice, garnished with fresh parsley. Pair with French bread for a complete Louisiana-inspired meal.

Lobster Mac and Cheese

Maine

To create perfect Lobster Mac and Cheese in a mini 2-quart crock pot, use fresh or frozen lobster meat for a rich, authentic taste. Pre-cook the macaroni and prepare the cheese sauce before layering them in the crock pot. Add the lobster meat during the last hour of cooking to keep it tender and avoid overcooking. Cook on low for 2-3 hours, allowing the flavors to meld. For a crunchy topping, add buttered breadcrumbs in the final 30 minutes. Serve hot with a garnish of parsley for a comforting and decadent Maine-inspired dish.

Ingredients

1 cup cooked macaroni, 4 oz lobster meat (cooked and chopped), 1/2 cup shredded sharp cheddar cheese, 1/4 cup grated Parmesan cheese, 1/2 cup whole milk, 1 tbsp butter, 1 tbsp all-purpose flour, 1/4 tsp garlic powder, 1/4 tsp paprika, 1/4 tsp salt, 1/4 cup breadcrumbs, 1 tsp fresh parsley (chopped).

Preparation

- Cook the macaroni according to package instructions and set aside.
- In a small saucepan, melt butter and whisk in flour to create a roux. Slowly add milk, stirring until smooth and thickened.
- Mix in cheddar cheese, Parmesan cheese, garlic powder, paprika, and salt until the cheese is melted and the sauce is smooth.
- Grease the mini 2-quart crock pot and add the cooked macaroni. Pour the cheese sauce over the macaroni and stir gently to combine.
- Add chopped lobster meat on top, ensuring it is evenly distributed.
- Sprinkle breadcrumbs over the top for a crispy texture.
- Cover and cook on low for 2-3 hours, checking to ensure the cheese is melted and bubbly.
- Serve hot, garnished with chopped parsley for a decadent Maine-inspired meal.

Old Bay Creamy Crab Soup

Maryland

To make the perfect Old Bay Creamy Crab Soup in a mini 2-quart crock pot, use fresh or canned crabmeat for the best flavor. Blend heavy cream and chicken broth for a rich base, and season generously with Old Bay for authentic Maryland flavor. Cook the soup on low for 4-5 hours to meld the flavors, stirring occasionally to prevent sticking. Add the crabmeat during the last 30 minutes of cooking to keep it tender. Garnish with parsley and serve with oyster crackers or crusty bread for a complete coastal meal. This hearty soup pairs perfectly with a crisp white wine.

Ingredients

6 oz crabmeat (fresh or canned), 1 cup chicken broth, 1/2 cup heavy cream, 1/4 cup diced onion, 1/4 cup diced celery, 1 tbsp butter, 1/2 tsp Old Bay seasoning, 1/4 tsp garlic powder, 1/4 tsp salt, 1/4 tsp black pepper, 1 tbsp fresh parsley (chopped).

Preparation

- Melt butter in a skillet and sauté onion and celery until softened, about 3 minutes.
- Transfer the sautéed vegetables to the mini 2-quart crock pot.
- Add chicken broth, heavy cream, Old Bay seasoning, garlic powder, salt, and black pepper. Stir to combine.
- Cover and cook on low for 4-5 hours, stirring occasionally to prevent sticking.
- Add crabmeat during the last 30 minutes of cooking, stirring gently to incorporate without breaking the crabmeat.
- Taste and adjust the seasoning as needed.
- Serve the soup hot, garnished with fresh parsley and a sprinkle of Old Bay seasoning. Pair with oyster crackers or crusty bread for a traditional Maryland-inspired meal.

Cranberry Maple Chicken

Massachusetts

To prepare Cranberry Maple Chicken for one or two people in a mini 2-quart crock pot, use boneless, skinless chicken thighs for their tenderness and flavor. Mix cranberry preserves and pure maple syrup for a rich glaze. Cook on low for 4-5 hours or high for 2.5-3 hours to allow the flavors to meld perfectly. Add fresh thyme and orange zest during the last 30 minutes for a burst of freshness. Serve with roasted potatoes or seasonal vegetables for a complete New England-inspired meal. This dish captures the essence of Massachusetts with its sweet and tangy flavor profile.

Ingredients

1/2 lb boneless, skinless chicken thighs, 1/4 cup cranberry preserves, 2 tbsp pure maple syrup, 1 tbsp orange juice, 1/4 tsp garlic powder, 1/4 tsp smoked paprika, 1/4 tsp salt, 1/4 tsp black pepper, 1 tsp fresh thyme (chopped), 1 tsp orange zest.

Preparation

- Season the chicken thighs with garlic powder, smoked paprika, salt, and black pepper.
- Place the chicken in the mini 2-quart crock pot.
- In a small bowl, mix cranberry preserves, maple syrup, and orange juice until smooth. Pour the mixture over the chicken.
- Cover and cook on low for 4-5 hours or high for 2.5-3 hours until the chicken is tender and fully cooked.
- During the last 30 minutes, sprinkle fresh thyme and orange zest over the chicken for added flavor.
- Use a spoon to baste the chicken with the glaze from the crock pot before serving.
- Serve warm with roasted potatoes or green beans, and garnish with additional thyme or orange zest for a festive touch.

Cherry BBQ Pork Loin

Michigan

For a tender and flavorful Cherry BBQ Pork Loin, use a lean pork loin cut and coat it generously with a mixture of cherry preserves and BBQ sauce. Sear the pork before adding it to the crock pot to lock in juices and develop a rich crust. Cook on low for 5-6 hours or high for 3-4 hours until the pork is tender. Baste the pork occasionally with the sauce for an enhanced flavor. Let the pork rest for a few minutes before slicing to retain its juices. Serve with mashed potatoes or roasted vegetables to complete this Michigan-inspired meal.

Ingredients

1/2 lb pork loin, 1/4 cup cherry preserves, 1/4 cup BBQ sauce, 1 tbsp apple cider vinegar, 1 tsp Dijon mustard, 1/4 tsp garlic powder, 1/4 tsp smoked paprika, 1/4 tsp salt, 1/4 tsp black pepper, 1 tsp fresh rosemary (chopped).

Preparation

- Season the pork loin with garlic powder, smoked paprika, salt, and black pepper.
- Heat a skillet over medium heat and sear the pork loin on all sides until golden brown, about 3 minutes per side.
- In a small bowl, mix cherry preserves, BBQ sauce, apple cider vinegar, and Dijon mustard to create a glaze.
- Place the pork loin in the mini 2-quart crock pot and pour the cherry BBQ glaze over it, ensuring it is evenly coated.
- Cover and cook on low for 5-6 hours or high for 3-4 hours until the pork is tender and fully cooked.
- Baste the pork with the sauce every hour to enhance its flavor.
- Let the pork rest for 5 minutes after cooking, then slice and serve with the remaining glaze spooned over the top.
- Garnish with fresh rosemary and serve alongside mashed potatoes or roasted asparagus for a Michigan-inspired meal.

Catfish Étouffée

Minnesota

For tender and flavorful Catfish Étouffée, use fresh or frozen catfish fillets and add them to the crock pot during the last hour of cooking to prevent overcooking. Sauté the holy trinity of Cajun cooking—bell peppers, onions, and celery—for a deeply flavorful base. Cook on low for 4-5 hours to allow the spices and broth to meld into a creamy sauce. Serve over white rice and garnish with parsley for a complete Mississippi-inspired meal. Adjust the heat level with cayenne pepper or hot sauce according to your taste preferences.

Ingredients

1/2 lb catfish fillets (cut into pieces), 1/2 cup diced onion, 1/4 cup diced bell pepper, 1/4 cup diced celery, 1 tbsp butter, 1 cup chicken broth, 1/4 cup heavy cream, 1/4 tsp garlic powder, 1/4 tsp paprika, 1/8 tsp cayenne pepper, 1/4 tsp salt, 1/4 tsp black pepper, 1 tbsp fresh parsley (chopped), 1 cup cooked white rice.

Preparation

- In a skillet, melt butter over medium heat and sauté onion, bell pepper, and celery until softened, about 3-4 minutes.
- Transfer the sautéed vegetables to the mini 2-quart crock pot.
- Add chicken broth, garlic powder, paprika, cayenne pepper, salt, and black pepper. Stir to combine.
- Cover and cook on low for 4-5 hours, stirring occasionally to prevent sticking.
- Add the catfish pieces during the last hour of cooking to ensure they cook through while remaining tender.
- Stir in heavy cream during the last 30 minutes to create a rich, creamy sauce.
- Serve the étouffée over cooked white rice, garnished with fresh parsley. Pair with cornbread or a green vegetable for a full Southern meal.

23

Kansas City BBQ Sliders

Mississippi

To make perfect Kansas City BBQ Sliders in a mini 2-quart crock pot, use a well-marbled pork shoulder for tender, juicy meat. Rub the pork with BBQ seasoning before cooking to infuse it with flavor. Cook on low for 6-7 hours or high for 3-4 hours until the meat easily shreds. Stir in your favorite Kansas City-style barbecue sauce in the last 30 minutes for a tangy, sweet finish. Serve on toasted slider buns with a dollop of coleslaw for added crunch. Keep warm in the crock pot for a crowd-friendly serving option.

Ingredients

1/2 lb pork shoulder (trimmed), 1/4 cup BBQ sauce, 1/4 cup chicken broth, 1 tsp BBQ seasoning, 1/8 tsp garlic powder, 1/8 tsp smoked paprika, 6 slider buns, 1/2 cup coleslaw (prepared), 2 tbsp pickle slices.

Preparation

- Rub the pork shoulder with BBQ seasoning, garlic powder, and smoked paprika.
- Place the pork in the mini 2-quart crock pot and pour chicken broth around it.
- Cover and cook on low for 6-7 hours or high for 3-4 hours until the pork is tender and easy to shred.
- Remove the pork from the crock pot and shred it using two forks. Return the shredded pork to the crock pot.
- Stir in BBQ sauce and mix well to coat the pork evenly. Cook for another 30 minutes on low.
- Toast slider buns if desired, and place a scoop of shredded BBQ pork on each bun.
- Top with coleslaw and add pickle slices for a tangy crunch. Serve immediately.

Venison and Barley Stew

Missouri

For a perfect Venison and Barley Stew, use tender venison chunks and pearl barley for a hearty texture. Brown the venison in a skillet before slow cooking to seal in the juices and enhance the flavor. Cook on low for 6-7 hours or high for 3-4 hours to ensure the venison becomes tender and the barley absorbs the rich broth. Add vegetables like carrots and celery for a balanced, hearty meal. Season generously with herbs like thyme and bay leaf for a deep, savory flavor. Serve with crusty bread for a warming, Montana-inspired dish that captures the rugged outdoors.

Ingredients

8 oz venison (cubed), 1/4 cup pearl barley, 1/2 cup diced carrots, 1/4 cup diced celery, 1/4 cup diced onion, 1 cup beef broth, 1/2 cup water, 1/4 tsp garlic powder, 1/4 tsp smoked paprika, 1/4 tsp salt, 1/4 tsp black pepper, 1 bay leaf, 1 tsp fresh thyme (chopped).

Preparation

- Season venison with garlic powder, smoked paprika, salt, and black pepper.
- Heat a skillet over medium heat and brown the venison on all sides for 3-4 minutes.
- Transfer the venison to the mini 2-quart crock pot.
- Add diced carrots, celery, onion, pearl barley, beef broth, and water. Stir to combine.
- Add a bay leaf and fresh thyme to enhance the flavor.
- Cover and cook on low for 6-7 hours or high for 3-4 hours until the venison is tender and the barley is cooked through.
- Remove the bay leaf before serving. Taste and adjust seasoning if needed.
- Serve hot with crusty bread for a satisfying Montana-inspired meal. Garnish with additional fresh thyme if desired.

Huckleberry BBQ Ribs

Montana

For perfectly tender ribs, use a 2-quart crock pot to evenly cook smaller portions. Remove the membrane from the back of the ribs before seasoning for better absorption of flavors. Use high-quality huckleberry preserves for an authentic Montana twist. Cook the ribs on low heat for 6-8 hours to achieve a fall-off-the-bone texture. Baste the ribs with additional barbecue sauce during the last hour for extra glaze. If you prefer a smoky flavor, finish the ribs under the broiler for 3-5 minutes after cooking. Serve with baked beans or cornbread for a complete Montana-inspired meal. Adjust seasoning to taste before serving.

Ingredients

1/2 rack baby back ribs, 1/4 cup huckleberry preserves, 1/4 cup barbecue sauce, 1 clove garlic (minced), 1/4 tsp smoked paprika, 1/4 tsp black pepper, 1/2 tsp salt, 1 Tbsp apple cider vinegar, 1/4 tsp cayenne pepper (optional), 1/4 cup water, 1/2 tsp olive oil.

Preparation

- Remove the membrane from the back of the ribs and pat them dry. Rub the ribs with a mixture of smoked paprika, black pepper, salt, and cayenne pepper if desired.
- Heat olive oil in a skillet and sear the ribs for 2-3 minutes on each side until lightly browned. Transfer to the crock pot.
- In a small bowl, mix huckleberry preserves, barbecue sauce, minced garlic, and apple cider vinegar. Pour the sauce mixture over the ribs.
- Add water to the crock pot to prevent drying and ensure a moist cooking environment. Cover with the lid.
- Set the crock pot to low heat and cook for 6-8 hours, occasionally spooning sauce over the ribs for an even glaze.
- Check the ribs for tenderness; they should easily pull apart with a fork. Adjust seasoning if necessary.
- For a caramelized finish, transfer the ribs to a baking sheet and broil for 3-5 minutes.
- Serve hot, garnished with fresh herbs, alongside baked beans or cornbread for a hearty Montana-style meal.

Corn and Cheese Casserole

Nebraska

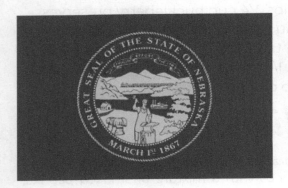

For the perfect Corn and Cheese Casserole in a mini 2-quart crock pot, use fresh or frozen corn for the best flavor and texture. Mix in a blend of cheddar and cream cheese to create a creamy base. Cook on low for 3-4 hours to allow the flavors to meld. Sprinkle breadcrumbs during the last 30 minutes to form a crispy topping. Stir occasionally to avoid sticking, and ensure the cheese is evenly melted. Garnish with fresh parsley for added color and serve warm. This dish pairs well with a green salad or grilled chicken for a satisfying Nebraska-inspired meal.

Ingredients

1 cup corn kernels (fresh or frozen), 1/4 cup diced onion, 1/4 cup shredded cheddar cheese, 2 oz cream cheese (softened), 1/4 cup milk, 1 tbsp butter, 1/4 cup breadcrumbs, 1/4 tsp garlic powder, 1/4 tsp smoked paprika, 1/4 tsp salt, 1/8 tsp black pepper, 1 tsp fresh parsley (chopped).

Preparation

- In a mixing bowl, combine corn, diced onion, cheddar cheese, cream cheese, milk, butter, garlic powder, smoked paprika, salt, and black pepper. Stir until well mixed.
- Transfer the mixture to the mini 2-quart crock pot and spread it evenly.
- Cover and cook on low for 3-4 hours, stirring occasionally to ensure the cheese melts evenly and the corn doesn't stick to the sides.
- In the last 30 minutes of cooking, sprinkle breadcrumbs over the top to create a crispy topping.
- Allow the casserole to cook uncovered for the final 10 minutes to let the breadcrumbs brown slightly.
- Garnish the casserole with fresh parsley before serving for a pop of color and added flavor.
- Serve warm as a main dish or a hearty side, pairing it with a protein or fresh salad for a complete meal.

Lamb and Potato Stew

Nevada

For a rich and satisfying Lamb and Potato Stew, use tender cuts of lamb shoulder and starchy potatoes for a creamy texture. Sear the lamb before adding it to the crock pot for extra flavor. Cook on low for 6-8 hours or high for 4-5 hours, allowing the ingredients to meld and the meat to become tender. Add vegetables like carrots and onions early, and season with rosemary and thyme for an aromatic finish. Serve the stew hot with crusty bread or a side of green vegetables for a Nevada-inspired hearty meal. Adjust seasoning to taste before serving.

Ingredients

8 oz lamb shoulder (cubed), 1 cup diced potatoes, 1/2 cup diced carrots, 1/4 cup diced onion, 1 cup beef broth, 1/2 cup water, 1 tbsp tomato paste, 1/2 tsp garlic powder, 1/4 tsp rosemary, 1/4 tsp thyme, 1/4 tsp salt, 1/8 tsp black pepper.

Preparation

- Season lamb cubes with garlic powder, rosemary, thyme, salt, and black pepper.
- Heat a skillet over medium heat and sear the lamb until browned, about 2-3 minutes per side.
- Transfer the lamb to the mini 2-quart crock pot.
- Add diced potatoes, carrots, and onion to the crock pot.
- In a small bowl, mix beef broth, water, and tomato paste until combined. Pour the mixture over the lamb and vegetables.
- Cover and cook on low for 6-8 hours or high for 4-5 hours until the lamb is tender and the vegetables are cooked through.
- Stir the stew occasionally to ensure even cooking and prevent sticking.
- Serve hot with crusty bread or a fresh salad, garnished with additional rosemary if desired.

Maple Pork and Sweet Potato Stew

New Hampshire

Live Free or Die

For a perfect Maple Pork and Sweet Potato Stew, use a well-marbled pork shoulder for tenderness and flavor. The sweetness of maple syrup pairs beautifully with the earthy flavors of sweet potatoes. Cook on low for 6-7 hours to fully tenderize the pork and allow the flavors to meld. Stir occasionally to ensure even cooking. Add a pinch of cinnamon or nutmeg for warmth. Serve with crusty bread or a simple green salad for a comforting New England-inspired meal. Adjust sweetness to taste, depending on the maple syrup's intensity.

Ingredients

1/2 lb pork shoulder (cubed), 1 cup diced sweet potatoes, 1/2 cup diced carrots, 1/4 cup diced onion, 1 tbsp pure maple syrup, 1 cup chicken broth, 1/4 tsp garlic powder, 1/4 tsp cinnamon, 1/4 tsp salt, 1/8 tsp black pepper, 1 tsp fresh parsley (chopped).

Preparation

- Season pork shoulder with garlic powder, cinnamon, salt, and black pepper.
- Heat a skillet over medium heat and brown the pork on all sides, about 3 minutes per side.
- Transfer the browned pork to the mini 2-quart crock pot.
- Add diced sweet potatoes, carrots, and onion to the crock pot.
- In a small bowl, mix chicken broth and maple syrup, then pour over the ingredients in the crock pot.
- Cover and cook on low for 6-7 hours or high for 3-4 hours until the pork is tender and the sweet potatoes are soft.
- Stir the stew occasionally for even cooking and to prevent sticking.
- Serve hot, garnished with fresh parsley, and pair with a slice of crusty bread for a hearty, New England-inspired meal.

Pork Roll and Egg Breakfast Sandwich

New Jersey

For a perfect Sausage and Bell Pepper Ragu, use high-quality Italian sausage for a rich, robust flavor. Slice the sausage and sear it before adding it to the crock pot to enhance its taste. Combine bell peppers, onions, and garlic for a vibrant base, and simmer with crushed tomatoes for a deep, hearty sauce. Cook on low for 4-5 hours to meld the flavors. Serve over pasta or polenta, garnished with fresh basil and Parmesan cheese. Stir occasionally to prevent sticking, and adjust seasoning to taste. This Italian-American dish captures the heart of New Jersey's culinary traditions.

Ingredients

6 oz Italian sausage (sliced), 1/2 cup diced bell peppers (mixed colors), 1/4 cup diced onion, 1 clove garlic (minced), 1 cup crushed tomatoes, 1/4 tsp garlic powder, 1/4 tsp smoked paprika, 1/4 tsp salt, 1/8 tsp black pepper, 1 tbsp olive oil, 1 tsp fresh basil (chopped), 1/2 cup cooked pasta (optional).

Preparation

- Heat olive oil in a skillet and sear the sausage slices until browned, about 2-3 minutes per side.
- Transfer the sausage to the mini 2-quart crock pot.
- Add diced bell peppers, onion, garlic, and crushed tomatoes to the crock pot.
- Stir in garlic powder, smoked paprika, salt, and black pepper, mixing thoroughly.
- Cover and cook on low for 4-5 hours or high for 2.5-3 hours until the vegetables are tender and the flavors are well combined.
- Stir occasionally to ensure even cooking and prevent sticking.
- Serve the ragu over cooked pasta or polenta, garnished with fresh basil and grated Parmesan cheese.
- Pair with garlic bread for a hearty New Jersey-inspired meal. Adjust seasoning before serving if needed.

Green Chile Chicken Stew

New Mexico

For a perfect Green Chile Chicken Stew, use fresh or frozen roasted green chiles for authentic New Mexican flavor. Add diced potatoes for texture and use chicken thighs for a tender, juicy result. Cook on low for 4-5 hours or high for 2.5-3 hours to allow the flavors to meld. Shred the chicken directly in the pot for convenience and stir in lime juice for a bright finish. Garnish with cilantro and serve with warm tortillas or crusty bread. Adjust the heat level with additional green chiles or a touch of hot sauce, depending on your preference.

Ingredients

1/2 lb chicken thighs (boneless), 1 cup diced potatoes, 1/2 cup diced green chiles (roasted), 1/4 cup diced onion, 1 cup chicken broth, 1/4 tsp garlic powder, 1/4 tsp cumin, 1/4 tsp smoked paprika, 1/4 tsp salt, 1/8 tsp black pepper, 1 tsp lime juice, 1 tbsp fresh cilantro (chopped).

Preparation

- Season chicken thighs with garlic powder, cumin, smoked paprika, salt, and black pepper.
- Place the chicken in the mini 2-quart crock pot and layer diced potatoes, green chiles, and onion on top.
- Pour chicken broth over the ingredients, ensuring everything is submerged.
- Cover and cook on low for 4-5 hours or high for 2.5-3 hours until the chicken is tender and fully cooked.
- Remove the chicken thighs, shred them with two forks, and return them to the crock pot. Stir to combine.
- Add lime juice and stir, tasting to adjust seasoning if needed.
- Garnish with chopped cilantro before serving.
- Serve hot with warm tortillas, lime wedges, and optional hot sauce for a Southwestern-inspired meal.

Reuben Casserole

New York

For a perfect Reuben Casserole, use high-quality corned beef and fresh rye bread for authentic deli flavors. Toast the rye bread cubes lightly before layering for extra texture. Layer corned beef, sauerkraut, Swiss cheese, and Thousand Island dressing for the classic Reuben taste. Cook on low for 2-3 hours or high for 1.5 hours to ensure the cheese melts and the layers meld together. Avoid overcooking to maintain the crispness of the bread cubes. Garnish with fresh parsley and serve hot for a comforting, New York deli-inspired meal. Pair with a side of dill pickles or a light salad.

Ingredients

6 oz corned beef (shredded), 1 cup rye bread cubes (toasted), 1/2 cup sauerkraut (drained), 1/4 cup Thousand Island dressing, 1/2 cup shredded Swiss cheese, 1 tbsp butter (melted), 1 tsp fresh parsley (chopped).

Preparation

- Lightly toast rye bread cubes and set them aside.
- Spread a thin layer of Thousand Island dressing on the bottom of the mini 2-quart crock pot.
- Layer shredded corned beef, sauerkraut, and Swiss cheese over the dressing.
- Add toasted rye bread cubes on top and drizzle with melted butter for added crispness.
- Cover and cook on low for 2-3 hours or high for 1.5 hours, allowing the cheese to melt and the flavors to meld.
- Stir gently if needed to ensure even cooking without breaking the bread cubes.
- Serve hot, garnished with fresh parsley, alongside dill pickles or a crisp green salad.
- Enjoy this hearty New York-inspired casserole as a main dish or comforting snack.

BBQ Sweet Potato Pulled Pork

North Carolina

For a flavorful BBQ Sweet Potato Pulled Pork, choose boneless pork shoulder for tender results. Sear the pork beforehand to enhance its flavor, and use a blend of BBQ sauce and spices to coat the meat evenly. Cook on low for 6-7 hours to ensure the pork shreds easily and the sweet potatoes become tender. Stir occasionally to prevent sticking. Use a fork to mash the sweet potatoes slightly before serving for a creamy texture. Garnish with parsley or green onions for a fresh finish. Serve with a side of cornbread or coleslaw for a true North Carolina-inspired meal.

Ingredients

1/2 lb pork shoulder (boneless), 1 cup diced sweet potatoes, 1/4 cup BBQ sauce, 1/4 cup chicken broth, 1/4 tsp garlic powder, 1/4 tsp smoked paprika, 1/4 tsp salt, 1/8 tsp black pepper, 1 tsp fresh parsley (chopped).

Preparation

- Season the pork shoulder with garlic powder, smoked paprika, salt, and black pepper.
- Heat a skillet over medium heat and sear the pork until browned, about 2-3 minutes per side.
- Transfer the pork to the mini 2-quart crock pot and layer diced sweet potatoes on top.
- Mix BBQ sauce and chicken broth in a small bowl, then pour the mixture over the pork and sweet potatoes.
- Cover and cook on low for 6-7 hours or high for 3-4 hours, until the pork is tender and easily shredded.
- Remove the pork, shred it with two forks, and return it to the crock pot. Stir to combine with the sauce.
- Mash the sweet potatoes slightly if desired, for a creamy consistency.
- Serve hot, garnished with chopped parsley, and pair with cornbread or coleslaw for a complete meal.

Creamy Potato Dumpling Soup

North Dakota

To create the perfect Creamy Potato Dumpling Soup, use starchy potatoes for a naturally thick texture. Incorporate pre-made dumplings or make your own for a hearty touch. Cook on low for 6-7 hours to ensure the potatoes are soft and the flavors meld together. Stir occasionally to prevent the dumplings from sticking to the pot. Adding cream towards the end of cooking will give the soup its signature rich and velvety texture. Garnish with fresh dill for a bright and earthy finish. Serve hot with crusty bread for a comforting, North Dakota-inspired meal that's perfect for chilly days.

Ingredients

1 cup diced potatoes, 1/2 cup pre-made dumplings, 1/4 cup diced onion, 1 clove garlic (minced), 1 cup chicken broth, 1/2 cup heavy cream, 1/2 tsp salt, 1/4 tsp black pepper, 1/4 tsp garlic powder, 1 tsp fresh dill (chopped).

Preparation

- In the mini 2-quart crock pot, combine diced potatoes, onion, minced garlic, chicken broth, salt, black pepper, and garlic powder. Stir well.
- Cover and cook on low for 5-6 hours until the potatoes are tender and easily pierced with a fork.
- Gently add the pre-made dumplings to the pot and stir them into the soup. Cover and continue cooking on low for another 1-2 hours.
- Stir in heavy cream during the last 30 minutes of cooking to create a rich and creamy texture.
- Taste and adjust seasoning with additional salt or pepper as needed.
- Garnish with freshly chopped dill for a burst of flavor and serve hot.
- Pair the soup with crusty bread or a light salad for a complete, satisfying meal.

Chili Mac and Cheese

Ohio

For the best Chili Mac and Cheese, use a mix of sharp cheddar and Monterey Jack for a creamy texture. Brown the ground beef before adding it to the crock pot to enhance the flavor. Let the dish cook on low for 3-4 hours or high for 1.5-2 hours to meld the chili and cheese flavors with the macaroni. Stir occasionally to prevent sticking and ensure the cheese is evenly distributed. Serve with chopped green onions or jalapeños for a spicy kick. Pair this comforting Ohio-inspired dish with cornbread for a complete meal.

Ingredients

4 oz ground beef, 1 cup cooked macaroni, 1/2 cup diced tomatoes, 1/4 cup kidney beans, 1/4 cup shredded cheddar cheese, 1/4 cup shredded Monterey Jack cheese, 1/4 cup diced onion, 1/4 cup chicken broth, 1/4 tsp chili powder, 1/4 tsp garlic powder, 1/8 tsp salt, 1/8 tsp black pepper, 1 tsp chopped green onions.

Preparation

- Brown the ground beef in a skillet over medium heat, breaking it into small pieces. Drain any excess fat.
- Transfer the cooked beef to the mini 2-quart crock pot.
- Add cooked macaroni, diced tomatoes, kidney beans, diced onion, chicken broth, chili powder, garlic powder, salt, and black pepper. Stir to combine.
- Layer shredded cheddar and Monterey Jack cheeses on top of the mixture.
- Cover and cook on low for 3-4 hours or high for 1.5-2 hours, stirring occasionally to ensure even melting and prevent sticking.
- Once the cheese is fully melted and the flavors have melded, garnish with chopped green onions.
- Serve hot with a side of cornbread or crackers for a complete and hearty meal. Adjust seasonings to taste before serving.

Cowboy Beef and Corn Casserole

Oklahoma

For a perfect Cowboy Beef and Corn Casserole, use lean ground beef to prevent excess grease. Brown the beef with onions before adding it to the crock pot to enhance the flavor. Layer sweet corn, black beans, and a seasoned cornbread mixture on top for a cohesive, hearty dish. Cook on low for 4-5 hours to allow the cornbread topping to bake evenly and meld with the filling. Avoid overcooking, as the cornbread may dry out. Garnish with fresh cilantro or diced jalapeños for a kick. Pair with a green salad or pickled vegetables for a well-rounded Oklahoma-inspired meal.

Ingredients

6 oz ground beef, 1/2 cup canned corn (drained), 1/4 cup black beans (rinsed), 1/4 cup diced onion, 1/2 cup cornbread mix, 1/4 cup milk, 1 egg, 1/4 tsp chili powder, 1/4 tsp garlic powder, 1/4 tsp salt, 1/8 tsp black pepper, 1 tsp fresh cilantro (chopped).

Preparation

- Heat a skillet over medium heat and brown the ground beef with diced onion until fully cooked, about 5 minutes. Drain excess grease.
- Transfer the beef and onion mixture to the mini 2-quart crock pot.
- Layer corn and black beans over the beef, spreading them evenly.
- In a small bowl, mix cornbread mix, milk, egg, chili powder, garlic powder, salt, and black pepper until smooth.
- Pour the cornbread batter over the layered ingredients in the crock pot.
- Cover and cook on low for 4-5 hours or high for 2-3 hours, until the cornbread is fully set and golden on top.
- Garnish with fresh cilantro before serving.
- Serve hot with a side of pickled jalapeños or a crisp green salad for a hearty Oklahoma-inspired meal.

Hazelnut and Mushroom Risotto

Oregon

To perfect Hazelnut and Mushroom Risotto in the crock pot, use Arborio rice for its creamy texture. Sauté mushrooms with garlic and onions before adding them to the crock pot for enhanced flavor. Add warm chicken or vegetable broth incrementally to maintain the rice's creamy consistency. Toasted hazelnuts provide a delightful crunch, while Parmesan cheese adds depth. Stir the risotto occasionally to prevent sticking and ensure even cooking. Cook on low for 2-3 hours, and garnish with parsley before serving. Pair with a crisp Oregon white wine for a meal that reflects the state's culinary heritage.

Ingredients

11/2 cup Arborio rice, 1/2 cup mushrooms (sliced), 1/4 cup diced onion, 1 clove garlic (minced), 1 cup chicken broth (warm), 1/4 cup toasted hazelnuts (chopped), 1/4 cup Parmesan cheese (grated), 1/2 tbsp olive oil, 1/4 tsp salt, 1/8 tsp black pepper, 1 tsp fresh parsley (chopped).

Preparation

- Heat olive oil in a skillet and sauté onions and garlic until fragrant, about 2 minutes. Add mushrooms and cook for another 3-4 minutes.
- Transfer the sautéed mixture to the mini 2-quart crock pot and add Arborio rice. Stir to coat the rice evenly.
- Gradually add 1/2 cup of warm chicken broth to the crock pot, stirring well. Cover and cook on low.
- After 1 hour, stir the mixture and add the remaining broth. Continue cooking on low for another 1-1.5 hours, stirring occasionally.
- Once the rice is tender and creamy, stir in grated Parmesan cheese and chopped hazelnuts. Adjust seasoning with salt and black pepper.
- Garnish with fresh parsley and serve immediately.
- Pair with a side salad or crusty bread for a complete, elegant meal.

Philly Cheesesteak Stuffed Peppers

Pennsylvania

To perfect Philly Cheesesteak Stuffed Peppers in the crock pot, use thinly sliced ribeye steak or deli roast beef for the most authentic flavor. Pre-cook the onions and bell peppers in a skillet for 2-3 minutes to release their natural sweetness and soften them before stuffing the peppers. For extra creaminess, blend provolone cheese with a little heavy cream before adding it to the mixture. Cook on low for 4-5 hours to let the flavors meld and the peppers become tender. You can serve these with a side of crispy fries for the full Philly experience.

Ingredients

2 large bell peppers (cut in half and cleaned), 6 oz ribeye steak (thinly sliced), 1/4 cup diced onion, 1/4 cup diced green bell pepper, 1/2 cup sliced mushrooms, 1/4 tsp garlic powder, 1/4 tsp black pepper, 1/4 tsp salt, 1/2 cup provolone cheese (shredded), 1/4 cup heavy cream, 1/4 cup beef broth, 1 tbsp olive oil.

Preparation

- Heat olive oil in a skillet over medium heat. Add onions, green bell pepper, and mushrooms. Sauté for 2-3 minutes until softened.
- Add thinly sliced ribeye steak to the skillet and cook for 2-3 minutes until browned. Stir in garlic powder, salt, and black pepper.
- Cut bell peppers in half and remove the seeds. Place them in the mini 2-quart crock pot.
- Stuff the peppers with the steak and vegetable mixture.
- In a small bowl, mix together beef broth, heavy cream, and shredded provolone cheese. Pour over the stuffed peppers.
- Cover and cook on low for 4-5 hours until the peppers are tender and the cheese is melted.
- Serve hot, garnished with additional cheese or fresh herbs as desired. Enjoy with fries for a classic Philly touch.

Corn and Clam Chowder

Rhode Island

To prepare Corn and Clam Chowder perfectly for 1-2 servings, use fresh, high-quality clams for the best flavor. Sauté the onions, celery, and garlic before adding them to the crock pot to release their natural sweetness. Be sure to use a good seafood stock to enhance the chowder's flavor, and add the clams in the last hour of cooking to prevent them from overcooking. Serve with a side of crunchy oyster crackers or warm bread. This chowder is best enjoyed immediately, but it can also be stored and reheated the next day for even richer flavor.

Ingredients

1/2 lb fresh clams (shucked and chopped), 1/2 cup corn kernels (fresh or frozen), 1/2 cup diced celery, 1/2 cup diced onion, 1 clove garlic (minced), 1 cup chicken broth, 1/2 cup heavy cream, 1 tbsp butter, 1/4 tsp smoked paprika, 1/4 tsp salt, 1/8 tsp black pepper, 1 tbsp fresh parsley (chopped).

Preparation

- In a skillet, melt the butter over medium heat. Add diced onions, celery, and minced garlic, sautéing until softened and fragrant, about 3 minutes. Stir occasionally to avoid burning.
- Transfer the sautéed vegetables into the mini 2-quart crock pot.
- Add the corn kernels (fresh or frozen), chicken broth, smoked paprika, salt, and black pepper. Stir to combine, ensuring that all ingredients are evenly distributed.
- Cover and cook the mixture on low for 3 hours, allowing the vegetables to cook through and the flavors to meld together. Stir occasionally to prevent sticking and ensure even cooking.
- After 3 hours, pour in the heavy cream and add the clams, being careful not to break them up too much. Stir gently to combine, then cover again.
- Continue cooking on low for another 1 hour, allowing the clams to cook through without becoming tough.
- Taste and adjust the seasoning with additional salt, pepper, or smoked paprika as desired.
- Once the chowder has thickened and the clams are tender, remove from the heat and let it sit for 5 minutes to rest.
- Garnish with fresh parsley and a sprinkle of smoked paprika, then serve hot with a side of crunchy oyster crackers or warm, crusty bread for dipping.
- For extra flavor, drizzle a little more heavy cream before serving. Enjoy this comforting and hearty Rhode Island-inspired chowder.

Lowcountry Crab Stew

South Carolina

For perfect Lowcountry Crab Stew, use fresh, high-quality crab meat to get the best flavor. Start by sautéing the onions and garlic to release their sweetness before adding to the crock pot. This stew benefits from a slow cook, allowing the flavors to develop, so be patient and cook on low for the full 4-5 hours. Adding the crab meat in the last 30 minutes prevents it from overcooking and becoming tough. Stir occasionally to keep the stew from sticking. Serve with cornbread or over rice to make it a complete and satisfying meal. This dish truly embodies the spirit of South Carolina's Lowcountry.

Ingredients

1/2 lb fresh crab meat, 1/2 cup diced onion, 1/4 cup diced bell pepper, 1/2 cup diced potato, 1/4 cup corn kernels (fresh or frozen), 1 cup chicken broth, 1/2 cup heavy cream, 1/4 tsp Old Bay seasoning, 1/8 tsp black pepper, 1 tbsp butter, 1 tbsp fresh parsley (chopped).

Preparation

- Heat butter in a skillet over medium heat. Add the diced onion, bell pepper, and garlic. Sauté for 2-3 minutes until softened.
- Transfer the sautéed vegetables into the mini 2-quart crock pot.
- Add the diced potato, corn kernels, chicken broth, Old Bay seasoning, and black pepper. Stir gently.
- Cover and cook on low for 4 hours. Stir occasionally.
- After 4 hours, add the fresh crab meat and heavy cream. Stir gently to combine.
- Cover and cook for another 30 minutes to heat through.
- Garnish with fresh parsley before serving.
- Serve hot with cornbread or over rice for a full Lowcountry meal.

Pheasant and Wild Rice Soup

South Dakota

To make Pheasant and Wild Rice Soup perfectly for 1 or 2 servings, it is important to cook the pheasant slowly to retain its tenderness. Use fresh wild rice for the best texture, and let it cook for the full time to absorb the flavors of the broth. For a creamier soup, add the cream towards the end of the cooking time, as it will thicken and add richness. Season generously with herbs like thyme and parsley, and adjust the salt to your taste. Serve with a slice of hearty bread to complete the dish.

Ingredients

1/2 lb pheasant meat (shredded), 1/4 cup wild rice, 1/4 cup diced carrots, 1/4 cup diced celery, 1/4 cup diced onion, 1/2 tsp dried thyme, 1/4 tsp black pepper, 1/2 tsp salt, 2 cups chicken broth, 1/4 cup heavy cream, 1 tbsp butter, 1 tbsp fresh parsley (chopped).

Preparation

- In a skillet, melt butter over medium heat. Add the diced onion, carrots, and celery. Sauté for 3-4 minutes until softened.
- Transfer the sautéed vegetables to the mini 2-quart crock pot.
- Add the pheasant meat, wild rice, thyme, black pepper, and salt. Stir to combine.
- Pour in the chicken broth, making sure the ingredients are fully submerged. Stir again.
- Cover and cook on low for 4-5 hours, stirring occasionally.
- After cooking, add the heavy cream and stir to combine.
- Let the soup cook for an additional 15-20 minutes.
- Garnish with fresh parsley and serve hot with a side of rustic bread.

BBQ Pulled Pork

Tennessee

To make the perfect BBQ Pulled Pork for 1 or 2 people, it's important to choose a tender cut like pork shoulder or butt. Slow cook on low for 6 to 8 hours to break down the fat and connective tissue for maximum flavor and tenderness. If you prefer a spicier flavor, opt for a BBQ sauce with a kick of heat, or add some extra hot sauce. Once the pork is fully cooked, shred it with two forks and mix in the BBQ sauce for a juicy, flavorful result. Serve on a bun with fresh coleslaw and pickles for the full experience.

Ingredients

1/2 lb pork shoulder or pork butt, 1/2 cup BBQ sauce, 1/4 cup chicken broth, 1/2 tsp smoked paprika, 1/4 tsp garlic powder, 1/4 tsp onion powder, 1/4 tsp salt, 1/4 tsp black pepper, 1/4 cup coleslaw, 2 pickle slices.

Preparation

- Trim any excess fat from the pork shoulder and place it in the crock pot.
- In a small bowl, mix the BBQ sauce, chicken broth, smoked paprika, garlic powder, onion powder, salt, and black pepper.
- Pour the sauce mixture over the pork, covering it completely.
- Cover the crock pot and cook on low for 6-8 hours or until the pork is tender and easily shreds.
- Remove the pork from the crock pot and shred it using two forks.
- Return the shredded pork to the sauce and mix well.
- Serve the pulled pork on a bun, topped with coleslaw and pickle slices.

Brisket and Pinto Bean Chili

Texas

For the perfect Texas Brisket and Pinto Bean Chili, ensure that the brisket is cooked slowly and thoroughly for maximum tenderness. Browning the brisket before placing it in the crock pot will add depth to the flavor. Use dried pinto beans for a richer taste, but remember to soak them overnight to avoid a longer cooking time. Adjust the spice level by adding more chili powder or cayenne pepper to suit your taste. Let the chili cook on low for 6-8 hours to allow all the flavors to meld together. Serve with cornbread for a complete meal.

Ingredients

1/2 lb brisket (cut into chunks), 1 can (15 oz) pinto beans (drained and rinsed), 1 can (14.5 oz) diced tomatoes, 1/2 cup onion (diced), 2 tbsp chili powder, 1 tsp garlic powder, 1/4 tsp cumin, 1/4 tsp smoked paprika, 1/2 tsp salt, 1/4 tsp black pepper, 1/4 cup beef broth, 1 tbsp olive oil, 1 tbsp fresh cilantro (chopped).

Preparation

- Heat olive oil in a skillet over medium heat. Brown the brisket chunks on all sides for 5-6 minutes.
- Transfer the browned brisket to the mini 2-quart crock pot.
- Add the pinto beans, diced tomatoes, onion, chili powder, garlic powder, cumin, smoked paprika, salt, black pepper, and beef broth to the crock pot.
- Stir the ingredients together to combine.
- Cover and cook on low for 6-8 hours or until the brisket is tender.
- Once cooked, shred the brisket with two forks.
- Stir everything together, garnish with chopped cilantro, and serve with cornbread.

Dutch Oven Beef Stew

Utah

For the perfect Dutch Oven Beef Stew, ensure that the beef is browned before adding it to the crock pot. This step locks in the flavor and creates a richer broth. Use a good quality beef broth and let the stew cook on low for 7 to 8 hours for the beef to become tender and flavorful. For added depth, consider using fresh herbs like thyme and rosemary. To thicken the stew, you can mash a few potatoes in the pot before serving. Serve with cornbread to make it a complete, comforting meal.

Ingredients

1/2 lb beef stew meat, 1/2 cup carrots (sliced), 1/2 cup potatoes (diced), 1/4 cup onion (chopped), 1 tsp garlic powder, 1/2 tsp dried thyme, 1/2 tsp rosemary, 1/2 tsp salt, 1/4 tsp black pepper, 1 cup beef broth, 1 tbsp tomato paste, 1 tbsp olive oil.

Preparation

- Heat olive oil in a large skillet over medium-high heat. Brown the beef stew meat on all sides for 5-6 minutes. This step helps to lock in the flavor.
- Transfer the browned beef to the crock pot.
- Add the sliced carrots, diced potatoes, chopped onion, garlic powder, thyme, rosemary, salt, and black pepper to the crock pot. Mix everything together so that the seasonings coat the vegetables and meat evenly.
- Stir the ingredients gently to combine.
- Add the beef broth and tomato paste to the pot. Stir to mix the tomato paste into the broth and vegetables.
- Cover the crock pot and set the heat to low. Cook for 7-8 hours or until the beef becomes tender and fully cooked.
- Once the stew is done, taste and adjust the seasoning if needed. Stir everything together and serve the stew hot with cornbread or crusty bread.

Maple and Apple Braised Chicken

Vermont

For the best results, start by browning the chicken in a skillet before transferring it to the crockpot. This enhances the flavor and gives the chicken a nice texture. Use high-quality maple syrup, as it's the star of this dish. Adjust the amount of maple syrup depending on how sweet you prefer the sauce. You can also add more apples for a fruity, slightly tangy note. Be sure to cook the chicken on low for 4-5 hours for tender meat. Lastly, serve the dish with mashed potatoes or crusty bread to soak up the rich sauce. Enjoy the fall flavors!

Ingredients

1 lb chicken thighs, 1 apple (sliced), 1/2 onion (sliced), 1/4 cup maple syrup, 1/2 cup chicken broth, 1 tbsp olive oil, 1 tsp fresh thyme, 1/4 tsp salt, 1/4 tsp pepper.

Preparation

- Heat olive oil in a skillet over medium heat. Season chicken thighs with salt, pepper, and thyme. Brown the chicken for 4-5 minutes on each side until golden brown.
- Transfer the browned chicken to the crockpot.
- Slice the apple and onion and add them to the crockpot with the chicken.
- Pour the maple syrup and chicken broth over the chicken and vegetables.
- Cover and cook on low for 4-5 hours or until the chicken is tender and fully cooked.
- Once done, check the seasoning and adjust salt and pepper to taste.
- Serve the maple and apple braised chicken over mashed potatoes or with crusty bread to soak up the sauce.
- Garnish with fresh herbs if desired, and enjoy the sweetness and savory flavors of Vermont in every bite.

Brunswick Chicken Stew

Virginia

To make the Brunswick Chicken Stew perfect for 1-2 servings, use bone-in chicken thighs or breasts for richer flavor. Browning the chicken before adding it to the crock pot will enhance the stew's depth. Be sure to chop the potatoes, carrots, and green beans into uniform sizes for even cooking. Use low-sodium chicken broth to avoid making the stew too salty, especially if adding canned corn or tomatoes. Cook on low for 6-7 hours or high for 3-4 hours, until the chicken is tender and shreds easily. For extra richness, stir in a dollop of sour cream just before serving.

Ingredients

1 lb chicken thighs (or breasts), 1 medium potato, peeled and diced, 1/2 cup corn kernels (fresh or frozen), 1/2 cup green beans, cut into 1-inch pieces, 1/2 cup diced tomatoes (with juice), 1/2 medium onion, chopped, 2 cloves garlic, minced, 2 cups low-sodium chicken broth, 1 tsp dried thyme, 1 tsp paprika, 1/2 tsp salt, 1/4 tsp black pepper, 1/4 tsp red pepper flakes (optional).

Preparation

- Heat a skillet over medium-high heat and brown the chicken thighs on both sides for 3-4 minutes. Transfer the chicken to the crock pot.
- Add the diced potatoes, corn, green beans, and diced tomatoes with their juice to the crock pot.
- In the same skillet, sauté the chopped onion and garlic until softened, about 3 minutes, then add to the crock pot.
- Pour the chicken broth into the crock pot, then season with thyme, paprika, salt, pepper, and red pepper flakes (if using).
- Stir the ingredients to combine, making sure the chicken is submerged.
- Cover and cook on low for 6-7 hours or high for 3-4 hours.
- Shred the chicken with two forks once it's cooked through, then stir back into the stew.
- Serve hot, garnished with optional fresh herbs or a dollop of sour cream if desired.

46

Apple and Sage Pork Roast

Washington

For the perfect Apple and Sage Pork Roast, select a well-marbled pork roast such as a boneless shoulder or loin to ensure tenderness and flavor. Searing the pork before placing it in the crockpot helps lock in juices and deepen the flavor. Use a tart variety of apples, like Granny Smith, for a balance of sweetness and acidity. Add fresh sage for a vibrant, earthy flavor that complements the apples. Cook on low for 6-7 hours to achieve the best texture, allowing the pork to become tender enough to shred. Serve with mashed potatoes or roasted vegetables for a complete meal.

Ingredients

1 lb pork roast, 2 medium apples, peeled, cored, and sliced, 1/2 medium onion, sliced, 2 cloves garlic, minced, 1 cup low-sodium chicken broth, 1 tbsp fresh sage, chopped, 1 tbsp olive oil, 1/2 tsp salt, 1/4 tsp black pepper, 1/4 tsp red pepper flakes (optional), 1 tbsp honey (optional).

Preparation

- Heat olive oil in a skillet over medium-high heat. Sear the pork roast for 2-3 minutes on each side until browned.
- Transfer the seared pork roast to the crockpot.
- Add the sliced apples, onion, and minced garlic to the crockpot around the pork.
- Pour the chicken broth over the pork and apples, ensuring they're evenly distributed.
- Sprinkle the fresh sage, salt, black pepper, and optional red pepper flakes over the ingredients.
- For extra flavor, drizzle honey over the apples if desired.
- Cover and cook on low for 6-7 hours or high for 3-4 hours, until the pork is tender and easily shreds.
- Once the roast is done, remove it from the crockpot and shred it with two forks.
- Stir the apple and onion mixture in the crockpot, and serve the shredded pork with the flavorful apple sauce.
- Enjoy your hearty meal with mashed potatoes or roasted veggies.

Pepperoni Roll Soup

West Virginia

To achieve the perfect Pepperoni Roll Soup in your crock pot for 1-2 people, start by evenly layering the ingredients to ensure even cooking. Choose fresh pepperoni for a richer flavor. You can add more vegetables, like bell peppers or onions, for extra taste. Keep an eye on the cooking time – typically 2 to 3 hours on high or 4 to 5 hours on low, but it's best to check the consistency and taste. If it's too thick, add a little more broth. For a crispy touch, serve with a slice of toasted bread or a mini pepperoni roll on top!

Ingredients

1/2 lb pepperoni, 1 cup diced potatoes, 1/2 cup diced onion, 1/4 cup diced bell pepper, 1 cup diced tomatoes, 1/2 cup shredded mozzarella cheese, 1 tbsp olive oil, 1/4 tsp garlic powder, 1/2 tsp salt, 1/4 tsp black pepper, 1/4 tsp red pepper flakes, 2 cups chicken broth, 1/4 cup grated Parmesan cheese, 1 tbsp chopped fresh parsley.

Preparation

- Begin by chopping the pepperoni into bite-sized pieces.
- Dice the onion, bell pepper, and potatoes into small cubes.
- Add the pepperoni, onions, bell pepper, and potatoes to your crock pot.
- Open the can of diced tomatoes and pour it into the crock pot, including the juice.
- Pour in the chicken broth, followed by the Italian seasoning, garlic powder, salt, and pepper. Stir to combine.
- Cover the crock pot and set it to cook on low for 4 to 5 hours or on high for 2 to 3 hours, until the potatoes are tender.
- Once the soup is done cooking, taste and adjust seasonings if needed.
- Stir in the mozzarella cheese until melted, then sprinkle the Parmesan on top just before serving.
- Serve hot with a slice of toasted bread or mini pepperoni rolls on the side for a true West Virginia experience.

Beer Brat Cheese Soup

Wisconsin

To make the Beer Brat Cheese Soup perfectly in a mini crock pot for one or two people, use high-quality bratwurst sausages, preferably fresh. Brown the sausages first to develop deep flavors before adding them to the crock pot. Ensure the cheese is melted slowly to avoid curdling, stirring gently as it melts. Cooking on low for 3 to 4 hours will allow the flavors to meld. If you prefer a thicker soup, blend a portion of the mixture before serving. Serve with a side of crusty bread to enjoy this hearty, comforting dish.

Ingredients

1 lb bratwurst sausage, 1 c shredded sharp cheddar cheese, 1 c heavy cream, 2 c chicken broth, 1 tbsp flour, 1/2 c beer, 1/2 tsp garlic powder, 1/4 tsp black pepper, 1/4 tsp salt, 1 tbsp unsalted butter.

Preparation

- Brown the bratwurst sausage in a skillet over medium heat, breaking them into small pieces as they cook.
- Transfer the sausage to the crock pot.
- Add the chicken broth, beer, and butter to the pot. Stir to combine.
- In a separate bowl, whisk the flour with a bit of the chicken broth to make a slurry, then add it to the crock pot to thicken the soup.
- Cook on low for 3-4 hours.
- After cooking, stir in the cream and shredded cheese.
- Cook for an additional 10 minutes, stirring occasionally until the cheese is fully melted.
- Season with garlic powder, salt, and pepper.
- Serve hot with toasted bread or croutons.

Beef and Vegetable Stew

Wyoming

For the best beef stew, use tougher cuts of beef like chuck roast, as it becomes more tender when cooked slowly in the crock pot. Brown the meat first to enhance its flavor, then layer it with root vegetables like carrots, potatoes, and parsnips. You can adjust the seasoning with fresh herbs like thyme and bay leaves for a warm, earthy flavor. For a rich stew, add a bit of red wine along with the broth. Cooking on low for 7-8 hours gives the flavors time to meld, and the beef will be melt-in-your-mouth tender.

Ingredients

11/2 lb beef stew meat, 1/2 c carrots (chopped), 1/2 c potatoes (diced), 1/4 c parsnips (sliced), 1/4 c onion (diced), 2 cloves garlic (minced), 1 tsp thyme, 1 bay leaf, 1/2 tsp black pepper, 1 tbsp tomato paste, 1 c beef broth, 1/2 c red wine (optional), 1 tbsp olive oil, 1/2 c frozen peas

Preparation

- Heat olive oil in a pan over medium-high heat. Brown the beef stew meat on all sides, then transfer to the crock pot.
- Add chopped carrots, diced potatoes, sliced parsnips, and diced onions to the crock pot.
- Mince the garlic and add it to the pot along with thyme, bay leaf, black pepper, and tomato paste.
- Pour in the beef broth and red wine (if using). Stir to combine everything.
- Cover the crock pot and cook on low for 7-8 hours until the beef is tender.
- About 30 minutes before serving, add the frozen peas and stir.
- Serve hot, optionally garnished with fresh herbs or crusty bread.

Pastrami and Swiss Cheese Dip

NY City

To ensure the Pastrami and Swiss Cheese Dip reaches peak perfection, cook it on low heat to slowly melt the cheese and allow all flavors to blend thoroughly. Stir the dip once or twice throughout the cooking process to ensure even consistency and prevent cheese from clumping. To maintain the perfect texture, add a small amount of cream if it appears too thick. For two servings, adjust cooking time accordingly, as smaller quantities may cook faster. Serve with toasted rye bread or crackers immediately while warm to enjoy the dip's creamy texture and flavors at their best.

Ingredients

4 oz pastrami, chopped, 1 cup shredded Swiss cheese, ½ cup cream cheese, softened, ¼ cup sour cream, 1 tbsp Dijon mustard, 2 tbsp finely chopped dill pickles, ½ tsp garlic powder, ¼ tsp ground black pepper.

Preparation

- Add the chopped pastrami, Swiss cheese, cream cheese, and sour cream to the crock pot.
- Stir in Dijon mustard, chopped dill pickles, garlic powder, and ground black pepper.
- Cover and cook on low for 1.5-2 hours until the cheese is completely melted and the mixture is creamy.
- Stir the mixture every 30 minutes to ensure even melting and prevent sticking.
- Once fully melted, taste and adjust seasoning with more mustard or pepper if desired.
- Serve the dip warm, garnished with extra chopped dill pickles.
- Arrange toasted rye bread or crackers on the side for dipping.
- Enjoy immediately for the best flavor and consistency.

Avocado Lime Chicken Soup

Los Angeles

For perfect results, ensure the chicken breasts are evenly sized to cook uniformly. Use fresh lime juice to brighten the flavor, and add it towards the end of the cooking time for a fresh, tangy note. Keep the avocado ripe but firm for the best texture. Cook on low to ensure the chicken remains tender, and check it after about 2 hours for a small crockpot. Taste and adjust the seasoning once it's done—salt and lime can bring all the flavors together beautifully. Remember, the key to this dish is its vibrant freshness, so garnish generously with cilantro right before serving

Ingredients

4 oz chicken breast, 1 cup chicken broth, 1/2 cup diced tomatoes, 1/4 cup diced onion, 1 garlic clove minced, 1 tsp chili powder, 1/2 tsp cumin, 1/4 tsp salt, 1/4 tsp black pepper, 1 tbsp lime juice, 1/2 avocado diced, 1 tbsp chopped cilantro.

Preparation

- Season chicken breast with salt, pepper, chili powder, and cumin, ensuring it's evenly coated for full flavor.
- Place the seasoned chicken breast into the mini 2-quart crockpot.
- Add the chicken broth, diced tomatoes, diced onion, and minced garlic into the crockpot, layering it over the chicken.
- Cover and cook on low for 3 to 4 hours, or on high for 1.5 to 2 hours, until the chicken is tender and cooked through.
- Remove the chicken breast from the crockpot, shred it using two forks, then return it to the crockpot, mixing it with the other ingredients.
- Stir in the lime juice, allowing it to blend with the soup for a few minutes.
- Add the diced avocado just before serving, to maintain its texture and color.
- Serve the soup hot, garnished with fresh chopped cilantro, and enjoy a taste of vibrant Los Angeles cuisine.

Italian Sausage and Pepper Stew

Chicago

For the perfect Italian Sausage and Pepper Stew for one or two people, use quality Italian sausage, ideally from your local butcher. This stew gains flavor over time, so allow it to simmer for the full cooking duration to enhance the flavors. If you like extra heat, add some crushed red pepper flakes. To prevent overcooking the peppers, add them halfway through the cooking process. Serve the stew with warm bread or a simple salad for a complete meal. If you're cooking for just one, you can easily freeze leftovers for up to a week in an airtight container—just thaw and reheat for a quick, delicious meal.

Ingredients

4 oz Italian sausage, 1 tbsp olive oil, 1/2 cup onion (chopped), 1/2 cup bell pepper (sliced), 1 clove garlic (minced), 1/4 tsp dried oregano, 1/4 tsp dried basil, 1/4 tsp salt, 1/8 tsp black pepper, 1/2 cup crushed tomatoes, 1/4 cup chicken broth, 1 tbsp tomato paste.

Preparation

- Heat a skillet over medium heat, add the olive oil, and cook the Italian sausage until browned. Drain excess grease and transfer the sausage to the crockpot.
- In the same skillet, sauté chopped onion and garlic until they become translucent, about 2-3 minutes. Transfer the cooked onions and garlic to the crockpot.
- Add the sliced bell pepper, crushed tomatoes, chicken broth, and tomato paste to the crockpot, then mix thoroughly.
- Sprinkle the oregano, basil, salt, and black pepper over the ingredients in the crockpot. Stir again to combine all flavors.
- Cover the crockpot and cook on low for 4-5 hours or on high for 2-3 hours until the sausage is tender and the flavors meld perfectly.
- Once done, taste the stew, and adjust salt and pepper if needed.
- Serve hot, topped with freshly chopped basil if desired. Pair with a slice of crusty bread for soaking up the flavorful sauce.

Beef Fajita Chili

Houston

To achieve the best flavor, sear the beef strips before adding them to the crockpot. This helps lock in the juices and adds a rich, smoky flavor. Use a combination of colorful bell peppers to make the dish more vibrant and nutritious. For an extra kick, add diced jalapeños or extra chili powder. If you're cooking for one, you can store leftovers in an airtight container in the fridge for up to three days. Pair with warm tortillas or serve over a bed of rice. Garnish with fresh cilantro and lime juice for a zesty finish that elevates the overall flavor of the chili.

Ingredients

8 oz beef sirloin (sliced into thin strips), 1 tbsp vegetable oil, 1/2 cup bell pepper (sliced), 1/4 cup onion (sliced), 1 clove garlic (minced), 1/2 tsp chili powder, 1/4 tsp cumin, 1/4 tsp smoked paprika, 1/4 tsp salt, 1/8 tsp black pepper, 1/2 cup diced tomatoes, 1/4 cup beef broth, 1/4 tsp Worcestershire sauce.

Preparation

- Heat a skillet over medium-high heat, add the vegetable oil, and sear the beef sirloin strips until browned. This should take about 3-4 minutes. Transfer the beef to the crockpot.
- In the same skillet, sauté the sliced onions and minced garlic for 2 minutes until they become fragrant. Transfer the onions and garlic to the crockpot.
- Add the sliced bell peppers, diced tomatoes, and beef broth to the crockpot. Stir well to combine.
- Sprinkle the chili powder, cumin, smoked paprika, salt, and pepper over the ingredients in the crockpot. Mix ev together to evenly distribute the spices.
- Add Worcestershire sauce to enhance the savo again to combine all the ingredients.
- Cover the crockpot and cook on low for 4-5 h 2-3 hours until the beef is tender and the flav
- Serve hot, garnished with fresh cilantro juice. Enjoy with warm tortillas or over ri

Sonoran Carne Asada Stew

Phoenix

To ensure the best flavor, always sear the
~~ada beef before adding it to the~~
~~the juices.~~

Ingredients

1/2 lb carne asada beef, 1 tbsp olive oil, 1/2 onion, diced, 1/2 bell pepper, chopped, 1 clove garlic, minced, 1/2 cup diced tomatoes, 1/4 cup beef broth, 1/2 tsp ground cumin, 1/4 tsp smoked paprika, 1/4 tsp chili powder, salt and pepper to taste, 1 tbsp lime juice, 1 tbsp chopped cilantro.

Preparation

- Heat the olive oil in a skillet, sear the carne asada beef until browned. Remove and set aside.
- In the same skillet, sauté onion, bell pepper, and garlic until softened.
- Add the beef, sautéed vegetables, diced tomatoes, and beef broth to the crock pot.
- Season with cumin, smoked paprika, chili powder, salt, and pepper.
- Cover and cook on low for 4 hours until the beef is tender.
- Stir in lime juice, then garnish with chopped cilantro before serving.
- Serve the stew warm, either with tortillas or over rice.

Philadelphia Pepper Pot Soup

Philadephia

To perfect Philadelphia Pepper Pot Soup, use fresh ingredients and layer flavors. Start by browning the beef for added depth. Tripe should be cleaned thoroughly and pre-boiled to soften. For a small 2-quart crock pot, halve the ingredients to fit, and add hot broth to kickstart cooking. Use fresh herbs like parsley for garnish right before serving. Stir occasionally to distribute ingredients evenly, and monitor the liquid level—add more broth if needed. For one person, divide ingredients by half again and freeze leftovers for convenience. Slow cooking on low enhances flavors; aim for 6–8 hours for the best results.

Ingredients

4 oz tripe, 1/4 lb beef stew meat, 1 medium potato (cubed), 1/4 cup diced onion, 1/4 cup diced celery, 1 small carrot (sliced), 1 clove garlic (minced), 1 tsp salt, 1/4 tsp black pepper, 1/4 tsp thyme, 1/4 tsp red pepper flakes, 2 cups beef broth, 1/4 cup heavy cream.

Preparation

- Rinse and pre-boil tripe for 10 minutes, then cut it into bite-sized pieces.
- In a skillet, sear the beef stew meat until browned, then transfer to the crock pot.
- Add tripe, potato, onion, celery, carrot, garlic, salt, pepper, thyme, and red pepper flakes to the crock pot.
- Pour beef broth over the ingredients, ensuring everything is submerged.
- Set the crock pot to low heat and cook for 6–8 hours until meat and vegetables are tender.
- During the last 30 minutes, stir in heavy cream to make the soup creamy.
- Adjust seasoning with additional salt or pepper if necessary.
- Serve hot, garnished with fresh parsley, and pair with crusty bread.

Pork Pozole Rojo

San Antonio

For perfect Pork Pozole Rojo, use fresh ingredients and a balanced combination of spices. Slow cooking tenderizes the pork and enhances flavors. In a 2-quart crock pot, ensure the pork is cut into small pieces to cook evenly. Blend the chile sauce until smooth for a silky broth. For one person, halve the recipe and adjust cooking time by an hour. Garnishes like radishes, lime wedges, and cilantro add freshness and crunch, so prepare them right before serving. Stir occasionally to prevent sticking, and ensure enough liquid to submerge the pork and hominy. Cooking on low heat for 6-7 hours ensures rich, authentic flavors.

Ingredients

1/2 lb pork shoulder (cubed), 1/2 cup dried hominy, 2 dried guajillo chiles, 1 clove garlic (minced), 1/4 onion (diced), 1 tsp oregano, 1/4 tsp cumin, 1 tsp salt, 1 cup chicken broth, 1/4 cup water, 1 Tbsp vegetable oil, fresh cilantro, radishes, lime wedges.

Preparation

- Rehydrate guajillo chiles by soaking them in hot water for 15 minutes, then blend into a smooth paste with water.
- Heat vegetable oil in a skillet, searing the pork until lightly browned. Transfer to the crock pot.
- Add hominy, onion, garlic, oregano, cumin, and salt to the crock pot.
- Stir in chicken broth and guajillo chile paste until evenly mixed.
- Cover and set the crock pot to low heat for 6-7 hours, stirring occasionally.
- Check the hominy for tenderness; if it's firm, extend cooking by 30 minutes.
- Taste and adjust seasoning as needed, adding a splash of water if the broth thickens too much.
- Serve in bowls, garnished with cilantro, radish slices, and lime wedges for a vibrant finish.

San Diego-Style Birria Tacos

San Diego

1542

To make perfect birria tacos, use a good-quality beef cut and allow the spices to infuse deeply during slow cooking. Use a 2-quart crock pot to ensure the broth is rich and flavorful. Sear the meat first to enhance flavor before adding to the slow cooker. For one person, halve the recipe and freeze leftover broth for later. Cook on low for 8 hours to make the beef tender and easy to shred. Assemble tacos just before serving to prevent sogginess. For dipping, strain the consommé to serve it clear. Always warm the tortillas to maintain the traditional texture and flavor.

Ingredients

1/2 lb beef chuck roast (cut into chunks), 1 dried guajillo chile, 1 dried ancho chile, 1 clove garlic (minced), 1/4 onion (diced), 1/4 tsp cumin, 1/4 tsp oregano, 1/8 tsp cinnamon, 1 tsp salt, 1 cup beef broth, 1/2 cup water, 2 corn tortillas, fresh cilantro, diced onion, lime wedges.

Preparation

- Rehydrate guajillo and ancho chiles by soaking them in hot water for 10 minutes, then blend with a little water into a smooth paste.
- Heat a skillet over medium-high heat and sear the beef chuck roast on all sides until browned, then transfer to the crock pot.
- Add the chile paste, garlic, onion, cumin, oregano, cinnamon, salt, beef broth, and water into the crock pot, stirring to combine.
- Cover and cook on low heat for 8 hours or until the beef is tender and falls apart easily.
- Remove the beef from the crock pot, shred it with two forks, and set aside. Strain the consommé to remove any solids.
- Dip corn tortillas into the consommé, then lightly fry in a skillet until slightly crispy.
- Fill the tortillas with shredded beef, garnished with cilantro and onion.
- Serve the tacos with consommé for dipping and lime wedges on the side.

Cowboy Beans with Bacon

Dallas

To perfect Cowboy Beans with Bacon, use fresh, high-quality ingredients and render the bacon until crispy for added depth. For a 2-quart crock pot, ensure the beans and sauce are well-mixed but leave some room to avoid overflowing. Adjust seasoning as the beans cook to balance the flavors. If making for one, halve the recipe and freeze any leftovers for convenience. Cook on low for a longer period (6-7 hours) to enhance the smoky flavors, stirring occasionally to prevent sticking. Serve with cornbread for an authentic Texan experience. For a sweeter kick, a tablespoon of brown sugar can be added during cooking.

Ingredients

4 oz dried pinto beans (soaked overnight), 3 slices bacon (chopped), 1/4 cup diced onion, 1 clove garlic (minced), 1/4 cup barbecue sauce, 1 tsp Worcestershire sauce, 1/2 tsp smoked paprika, 1/4 tsp chili powder, 1 tsp salt, 1/4 tsp black pepper, 1 1/2 cups water.

Preparation

- Rinse soaked pinto beans and set aside. Chop the bacon into small pieces and cook in a skillet until crispy, then transfer to the crock pot.
- Use the bacon grease in the skillet to sauté onions and garlic until softened, about 2-3 minutes. Add them to the crock pot.
- Combine the beans, barbecue sauce, Worcestershire sauce, smoked paprika, chili powder, salt, and pepper in the crock pot.
- Pour water over the mixture, ensuring the beans are fully submerged. Stir well to combine all ingredients.
- Set the crock pot to low heat and cook for 6-7 hours, stirring occasionally.
- Check the beans for tenderness; if they are firm, cook for an additional 30-60 minutes.
- Adjust seasoning to taste before serving, adding more salt or barbecue sauce if desired.
- Serve hot with cornbread and garnish with reserved crispy bacon for added texture and flavor.

Garlic Herb Chicken and Vegetables

San Jose

For the perfect Garlic Herb Chicken and Vegetables, use fresh, high-quality ingredients. Marinate the chicken beforehand for deeper flavor. A 2-quart crock pot works best for even cooking with minimal liquid, letting the chicken roast rather than stew. Layer the vegetables under the chicken so they absorb its juices. Cook on low for 6-7 hours for tender chicken and perfectly cooked vegetables. Adjust seasoning midway for balance. If making for one person, halve the recipe and monitor closely to avoid overcooking. To enhance the dish, finish with a squeeze of lemon juice and a sprinkle of fresh parsley right before serving.

Ingredients

2 chicken thighs (bone-in, skin-on), 1/2 lb baby potatoes (halved), 1/2 cup baby carrots, 1/2 cup green beans, 2 cloves garlic (minced), 1 tsp dried thyme, 1/2 tsp rosemary, 1/4 tsp paprika, 1 tsp salt, 1/4 tsp black pepper, 1 Tbsp olive oil, 1/4 cup chicken broth.

Preparation

- Season the chicken thighs with thyme, rosemary, paprika, salt, and pepper. Rub with olive oil and set aside.
- Layer the baby potatoes, carrots, and green beans in the bottom of the crock pot. Sprinkle minced garlic over the vegetables.
- Place the seasoned chicken thighs on top of the vegetables, ensuring they are not submerged.
- Pour chicken broth around the edges to add moisture without covering the ingredients.
- Cover and cook on low for 6-7 hours or until the chicken is tender and reaches an internal temperature of 165°F.
- Check halfway through and stir the vegetables to ensure even cooking. Add more seasoning if needed.
- Before serving, transfer the chicken to a broiler-safe dish and broil for 3-5 minutes to crisp the skin.
- Garnish with fresh parsley and serve warm, paired with crusty bread or a light salad.

Black Bean and Brisket Chili

Austin

CITY OF AUSTIN

To make the perfect Black Bean and Brisket Chili, use well-marbled brisket for tender results. A 2-quart crock pot is ideal for a small batch, ensuring the flavors meld perfectly. Sear the brisket beforehand to enhance its smoky flavor. For a spicier kick, add a pinch of cayenne pepper or diced jalapeño. Stir occasionally to distribute the spices evenly and check the liquid level, adding broth if it thickens too much. If making for one person, halve the ingredients and adjust seasoning to taste. Serve with cornbread or tortilla chips for a hearty Austin-inspired meal, and garnish with sour cream or shredded cheese.

Ingredients

1/2 lb brisket (cut into chunks), 1/2 cup black beans (soaked overnight), 1/4 cup diced onion, 1 clove garlic (minced), 1 cup diced tomatoes (canned), 1/4 cup beef broth, 1 tsp chili powder, 1/2 tsp smoked paprika, 1/4 tsp cumin, 1 tsp salt, 1/4 tsp black pepper, 1/4 tsp red pepper flakes, 1 tsp olive oil.

Preparation

- Heat olive oil in a skillet and sear the brisket chunks on all sides until browned, then transfer to the crock pot.
- Rinse and drain the soaked black beans, adding them to the crock pot with the brisket.
- Add diced onions, minced garlic, canned tomatoes, beef broth, chili powder, smoked paprika, cumin, salt, black pepper, and red pepper flakes.
- Stir the mixture to combine all ingredients evenly, ensuring the brisket and beans are submerged in the liquid.
- Cover the crock pot and set it to low heat. Cook for 6–8 hours, stirring occasionally to prevent sticking.
- Check the brisket for tenderness; it should easily fall apart when done. Adjust seasoning as needed.
- Garnish with fresh cilantro, diced onions, and a dollop of sour cream before serving.
- Serve hot with cornbread, tortilla chips, or warm tortillas for a complete meal.

Grouper and Citrus Chowder

Jacksonville

For the best Grouper and Citrus Chowder, use fresh, high-quality grouper and citrus to highlight the coastal flavors. A 2-quart crock pot works well for small portions. Sear the grouper lightly beforehand for added flavor without overcooking. Add citrus zest towards the end of cooking to preserve its fresh aroma. Stir occasionally to evenly distribute the cream and ensure the chowder does not separate. For one person, halve the ingredients and monitor cooking times closely to avoid overcooking the fish. Serve immediately with a wedge of lemon and crusty bread to soak up the creamy broth. Always taste and adjust seasoning as needed.

Ingredients

16 oz grouper (cut into chunks), 1/2 cup diced potatoes, 1/4 cup diced carrots, 1/4 cup diced celery, 1/4 cup diced onion, 1 cup fish stock, 1/4 cup heavy cream, 1 tsp lemon zest, 1/2 tsp salt, 1/4 tsp black pepper, 1 Tbsp olive oil, 1/4 tsp smoked paprika, fresh parsley for garnish.

Preparation

- Heat olive oil in a skillet and sear the grouper chunks for 1-2 minutes per side until lightly browned, then set aside.
- Add diced potatoes, carrots, celery, and onions to the crock pot, layering them evenly.
- Pour in fish stock and season with salt, pepper, and smoked paprika. Stir gently to combine.
- Cover and cook on low for 4-5 hours, stirring occasionally to ensure the vegetables cook evenly.
- During the last 30 minutes, stir in heavy cream and lemon zest, and carefully add the seared grouper to the crock pot.
- Taste the chowder and adjust seasoning with additional salt or pepper if needed.
- Serve hot in bowls, garnished with fresh parsley and a wedge of lemon for added freshness.
- Pair with crusty bread or crackers for a complete, hearty meal that reflects Jacksonville's coastal flavors.

Gumbo with Andouille Sausage and Chicken

New Orleans

For the perfect gumbo, use a dark roux as the base for rich flavor. Sauté the vegetables before adding them to the crock pot to enhance their sweetness. A 2-quart crock pot is perfect for two servings, with even cooking and a well-balanced broth-to-ingredient ratio. Stir occasionally to prevent ingredients from sticking. For one person, halve the recipe and store leftovers for later. Always cook the sausage and chicken beforehand to avoid a greasy texture in the final dish. Serve over freshly cooked white rice for an authentic New Orleans experience. Garnish with green onions and adjust seasoning as needed.

Ingredients

1/2 lb chicken thighs (cut into chunks), 3 oz Andouille sausage (sliced), 1/4 cup diced onion, 1/4 cup diced green bell pepper, 1/4 cup diced celery, 1 clove garlic (minced), 2 Tbsp all-purpose flour, 2 Tbsp vegetable oil, 1 cup chicken broth, 1/4 cup diced tomatoes, 1/2 cup okra (sliced), 1/2 tsp Cajun seasoning, 1/4 tsp thyme, 1/4 tsp salt, 1/8 tsp black pepper, cooked white rice.

Preparation

- In a skillet, heat vegetable oil and whisk in the flour. Cook over medium heat, stirring constantly, until the roux turns a deep golden brown, then transfer to the crock pot.
- In the same skillet, cook Andouille sausage slices until browned. Remove and set aside.
- Sauté the chicken chunks in the skillet until lightly browned, then transfer to the crock pot.
- Add diced onion, green bell pepper, celery, garlic, okra, and diced tomatoes to the crock pot. Stir to mix evenly with the roux.
- Pour in chicken broth and season with Cajun seasoning, thyme, salt, and black pepper. Stir to combine.
- Cover and cook on low for 6-7 hours, stirring occasionally.
- Check the chicken for doneness and adjust seasoning if necessary. Add cooked sausage back to the pot during the final 30 minutes.
- Serve hot over white rice, garnished with green onions, for a flavorful New Orleans meal.

Chinatown Five-Spice Beef Stew

San Francisco

To achieve perfection, use fresh ingredients and a well-balanced blend of spices. Brown the beef chunks beforehand to enhance flavor. A 2-quart crock pot is ideal for small portions and ensures even cooking. Add the bok choy in the final hour to prevent overcooking. Stir occasionally to distribute the spices and check the broth consistency. For a thicker stew, mix a small amount of cornstarch with water and stir it in during the last 30 minutes. If making for one person, halve the ingredients. Serve the stew hot with steamed rice and garnish with green onions for an authentic Chinatown experience.

Ingredients

1/2 lb beef stew meat (cut into chunks), 1/4 cup sliced carrots, 1/4 cup diced onion, 1/2 cup bok choy (chopped), 1 clove garlic (minced), 1 tsp Chinese five-spice powder, 1 Tbsp soy sauce, 1 Tbsp oyster sauce, 1 tsp sesame oil, 1 cup beef broth, 1/4 tsp salt, 1/8 tsp black pepper, 1/2 tsp cornstarch (optional).

Preparation

- Heat sesame oil in a skillet and sear the beef chunks until browned on all sides, then transfer to the crock pot.
- Add carrots, onions, and minced garlic to the crock pot, layering them evenly with the beef.
- In a small bowl, mix beef broth, soy sauce, oyster sauce, Chinese five-spice powder, salt, and black pepper. Pour the mixture over the beef and vegetables.
- Stir gently to combine all ingredients. Cover and set the crock pot to low heat.
- Cook for 6-7 hours, stirring occasionally to distribute the flavors and check the liquid level.
- During the last hour of cooking, add the chopped bok choy to the crock pot and stir gently.
- If a thicker stew is desired, mix cornstarch with a tablespoon of water and stir it into the crock pot during the final 30 minutes.
- Serve the stew hot with steamed rice, garnished with sliced green onions for added freshness.

Rocky Mountain Vegetable Soup

Denver

For the perfect Rocky Mountain Vegetable Soup, use fresh, seasonal vegetables for vibrant flavors. A 2-quart crock pot works well for a small batch, ensuring balanced cooking. Cut the vegetables into even pieces to cook uniformly, and sauté onions and garlic beforehand for added depth. Use vegetable broth for a light base, but you can enrich the flavor with a splash of white wine. Add tender vegetables like green beans during the last hour to maintain texture. For one person, halve the recipe and save leftovers for the next day—it tastes even better. Serve with crusty bread for a wholesome Denver-inspired meal.

Ingredients

1/2 cup diced potatoes, 1/4 cup sliced carrots, 1/4 cup green beans (trimmed), 1/4 cup corn kernels, 1/4 cup diced onion, 1 clove garlic (minced), 1 cup vegetable broth, 1/4 tsp dried thyme, 1/4 tsp dried oregano, 1/2 tsp salt, 1/4 tsp black pepper, 1 Tbsp olive oil, 1/4 tsp smoked paprika.

Preparation

- Heat olive oil in a skillet and sauté the diced onion and minced garlic until fragrant, about 2 minutes, then transfer to the crock pot.
- Add diced potatoes, sliced carrots, corn kernels, and vegetable broth to the crock pot.
- Season with thyme, oregano, smoked paprika, salt, and black pepper, stirring gently to combine all ingredients.
- Cover and cook on low heat for 5-6 hours, or until the potatoes and carrots are tender.
- During the last hour of cooking, add the green beans to prevent them from becoming too soft.
- Stir the soup occasionally to distribute flavors evenly and check the seasoning, adjusting salt or pepper as needed.
- Once done, serve the soup hot in bowls, garnished with fresh herbs if desired.
- Pair with a slice of crusty bread or a warm biscuit for a comforting Rocky Mountain experience.

Rainy-Day Lentil Soup

Seattle

Use high-quality lentils for consistent cooking and a hearty texture. A 2-quart crock pot ensures a balanced portion for one or two people. Sauté onions, celery, and carrots beforehand to enhance their natural sweetness and add depth to the soup. Stir occasionally to evenly distribute the flavors and check the lentils' doneness. Add delicate greens like spinach in the last hour to maintain freshness. For a thicker soup, mash some lentils against the side of the pot before serving. Pair with crusty sourdough bread for a complete, comforting meal. If cooking for one, halve the ingredients and freeze leftovers for a future rainy day.

Ingredients

1/2 cup dry lentils, 1/4 cup diced carrots, 1/4 cup diced celery, 1/4 cup diced onion, 1 cup vegetable broth, 1 cup water, 1 clove garlic (minced), 1/4 tsp dried thyme, 1/4 tsp dried oregano, 1/4 tsp smoked paprika, 1 tsp olive oil, 1/4 tsp salt, 1/8 tsp black pepper, 1/2 cup fresh spinach.

Preparation

- Heat olive oil in a skillet and sauté diced onion, celery, and carrots for 2-3 minutes until softened, then transfer to the crock pot.
- Rinse the dry lentils thoroughly and add them to the crock pot.
- Add minced garlic, thyme, oregano, smoked paprika, salt, and black pepper, followed by vegetable broth and water. Stir gently to combine.
- Cover and cook on low heat for 6-7 hours, stirring occasionally to ensure even cooking and prevent sticking.
- During the last hour, stir in the fresh spinach to allow it to wilt and infuse the soup with additional flavor.
- Taste and adjust seasoning, adding more salt or black pepper if needed. For a creamier texture, mash some lentils against the pot's sides.
- Serve the soup hot, paired with crusty sourdough bread or crackers, for a warming and hearty meal on a rainy day.
- Garnish with a drizzle of olive oil or fresh herbs if desired.

Southern Collard Greens with Smoked Turkey

Atlanta

To make tender and flavorful collard greens, wash the greens thoroughly to remove any grit. A 2-quart crock pot is ideal for small servings, ensuring even cooking and deep flavors. Use smoked turkey wings or drumsticks for authentic Southern taste. Add a touch of apple cider vinegar during cooking to enhance the flavors. Stir occasionally to ensure the greens cook evenly and adjust seasoning as needed. For one serving, halve the ingredients and save leftovers for the next day—it tastes even better. Serve hot with cornbread to soak up the savory broth, making it a complete Southern comfort meal.

Ingredients

1/2 lb fresh collard greens (washed and chopped), 1/4 lb smoked turkey (wings or drumsticks), 1 cup chicken broth, 1/4 cup diced onion, 1 clove garlic (minced), 1 tsp apple cider vinegar, 1/2 tsp salt, 1/4 tsp black pepper, 1/4 tsp crushed red pepper flakes, 1 Tbsp olive oil, 1/2 tsp sugar.

Preparation

- Heat olive oil in a skillet and sauté diced onion and minced garlic until fragrant, about 2 minutes. Transfer to the crock pot.
- Wash and chop the collard greens, removing thick stems, and add them to the crock pot.
- Place smoked turkey on top of the greens and pour chicken broth over the mixture.
- Add apple cider vinegar, salt, black pepper, crushed red pepper flakes, and sugar. Stir gently to combine.
- Cover the crock pot and set it to low heat. Cook for 6-7 hours, stirring occasionally to ensure even cooking.
- Check the smoked turkey for tenderness; it should easily pull apart. Remove any bones if desired.
- Taste and adjust seasoning, adding more salt or vinegar as needed for flavor balance.
- Serve hot with cornbread, garnished with extra crushed red pepper flakes for a touch of heat.

Cherry Blossom BBQ Pulled Pork

Washington DC

To make tender and flavorful pulled pork, use a well-marbled pork shoulder. A 2-quart crock pot is ideal for smaller portions, ensuring even cooking. For the cherry flavor, use high-quality cherry preserves or fresh cherries blended into the sauce. Cook the pork on low heat for 8 hours to allow the flavors to meld and the meat to shred easily. Stir occasionally to coat the pork with sauce evenly. For one serving, halve the ingredients and freeze leftovers for later. Serve on a bun with coleslaw or alongside cornbread to capture the essence of this Washington, D.C.-inspired dish.

Ingredients

1/2 lb pork shoulder, 1/4 cup cherry preserves, 1/4 cup barbecue sauce, 1/4 cup diced onion, 1 clove garlic (minced), 1/2 tsp smoked paprika, 1/4 tsp cayenne pepper, 1/2 tsp salt, 1/4 tsp black pepper, 1 Tbsp apple cider vinegar, 1/4 cup water, 1/2 tsp olive oil.

Preparation

- Rub the pork shoulder with smoked paprika, cayenne pepper, salt, and black pepper. Heat olive oil in a skillet and sear the pork on all sides until browned, then transfer to the crock pot.
- In a small bowl, mix cherry preserves, barbecue sauce, apple cider vinegar, and water. Pour the mixture over the pork in the crock pot.
- Add diced onion and minced garlic around the pork, ensuring even distribution of flavors.
- Cover the crock pot and set it to low heat. Cook for 8 hours, turning the pork occasionally and spooning sauce over it.
- After cooking, shred the pork using two forks directly in the crock pot, mixing it well with the sauce.
- Adjust seasoning to taste and allow the pork to soak in the sauce for an additional 10 minutes on the warm setting.
- Serve the pulled pork on buns, alongside coleslaw, or with cornbread for a hearty and flavorful meal.
- Garnish with a sprinkle of chopped parsley or fresh cherries for a decorative touch.

Made in the USA
Monee, IL
14 December 2024